YOUR SECRET SUPERPOWER

Tame Fear to Thrive

BRIAN MUKA

Muka, Brian, Your Secret Superpower: Tame Fear to Thrive

Published by KWE Publishing, www.kwepub.com

ISBN (paperback) 978-0-9997254-7-4, ISBN (ebook) 978-1-950306-05-3

Library of Congress Catalog Number: 2019938333

Brian Muka

Contact Brian at https://www.Fearsherpa.com/ and begin to command Fear!

STOP!!!!!

Please, before reading further, claim your resources I built for you.

Click www.yoursecretsuperpowerbook.com and download your free resources.

This content will help you apply the powerful and effective tools, techniques, and mindset to your life immediately.

Dedicated to the team that rescued me from my avalanche. I love you so much, and dedicate this Fear Sherpa work to aiding others in their climb back to the light. I couldn't have done any of this without your love and your belief. You believed in me when I didn't believe in myself.

FOREWORD

Inside of a large athletics stadium lies a Long Jump runway, and at the end of this runway, is a pit full of soft, welcoming sand. Imagine standing on this runway, and off to your left are stands full of antsy spectators waiting for you to sprint forward toward the sand. You take off and gradually accelerate. The crowd roars. That acceleration leads to top speed, and you're now flying down the track. At the appropriate time, you take your last stride, and jump! You have made a commitment to fly, and your body soars through the air. Gravity reigns true as you begin to fall toward earth. The crowd erupts as you make a successful landing in the sand pit.

Now, I want you to relive this scenario and imagine how it might play out if you were blind. Would you be able to do it? Could you commit to running, and then jumping, without your eyesight?

I am a Paralympic Long Jumper for Team USA, and I compete without the ability to see. I have a guide who stands at the takeoff board and he claps and yells, giving me an auditory reference as to where I should jump from. I remember how many strides to take and count them in my head. At the appropriate stride, I jump and soar through the air. In Paralympic competition, competitors are actually instructed to wear a blindfold to ensure everyone is on an equal playing field. How's that for irony?

For the past fourteen years I have been fortunate enough to wear the red, white and blue in many competitions on the global stage. I have won multiple Paralympic medals, world-champion titles, and national championships. I am the current World Record Holder in the Long Jump for totally blind athletes with a leap of twenty-two feet one inch.

The average person seems to believe that I live a life consumed by Fear. I get questions like, "Do you feel alone?" and, "Isn't it frightening navigating this world without your eyesight?" From the outside looking in, the average person believes that I must feel overwhelming anguish created by the darkness that has fallen upon my eyes. That is far from the truth.

In this book lies the heart of a powerful statement from Napoleon Hill,

> **"Every adversity, every failure, every heartache carries with it the seed of an equal or greater benefit."**

Initially, I chose to be coddled and comforted by Fear. I allowed fearful thoughts to fester and grow within my imagination. As Brian mentions, these thoughts are always worse than the actual consequences. I would eventually gain immense strength and power by standing boldly in the face of Fear and conquering it. I am grateful for blindness because through it, a vision of success for my life was born.

Is there an overpowering force that is keeping you from maximizing your potential? Is Fear safeguarding endless treasure that is especially for you? Are you willing to take the steps that will help you harness Fear and channel it in a way that will lead to abundant growth and personal achievement? If you answered, "Yes," to these questions, then this book is for you.

Within these pages, lies the key that will help you unlock a future of self-discovery and mastery. Brian's personal account is one that will introduce you to his failures, successes, vulnerabilities, and resilience. This guidebook will take you by the hand and lead you through uncomfortable moments and challenges in life. It will also scale the mountain with you and celebrate your successes once you reach the pinnacle.

Fear Sherpa will help you identify and embrace your vulnerabilities, and reveal the resilience inside of you. Within these chapters are action steps that you can implement and benefit from at this very moment.

As an eight-year-old boy, I was diagnosed with recurrent retina detachments. Thirteen operations failed to stabilize what little sight I had, and after the last procedure, my doctor said that there was nothing else he could do. I was told that I would eventually lose my sight. From that day forward, I would come home, go through my daily routine, fall asleep, and wake the next morning only to see less than what I did the day before.

The day finally arrived when I woke up, and I couldn't see anything. I felt defeated, I felt isolated, I felt disconnected. With the help of my mom, my first track and field coach, and others, I was able to rise from this sunken place and emerge victorious. You see, when you are faced with the most unbearable adversities, don't fret, because on the other side is gold. I have navigated through the darkness for years, and I am able to do it with much confidence because of the faith that runs through my soul and fuels my body. I believe that every adversity contains a seed of an equal or greater benefit, and I truly believe this is the same for you. The elements found within this book will help you ascend beyond your challenges toward a world of pure bliss.

Now, return to the athletics stadium. I am visualizing you standing on the long jump runway in front of thousands of expectant eyes. You take a moment to slide the blindfold onto your face. You can see nothing, but I can see you as you take that first stride. Your feet drive into the ground, accelerating your body forward down the runway. You move faster, and faster, and faster until you reach top speed. The crowd watches in excitement. At the right moment, you jump, and fly through the air. This is a feeling that I have come to love, running in the midst of darkness, and leaping into the abyss.

I'm certain that this book will help you shift your mindset to a space where you will welcome this challenge. You will be equipped with the skills and tools useful in facing Fear head-on. You too will make the decision to run in darkness on the basis of knowing that ahead, there is overwhelming light waiting. Without even thinking, you will make the decision to jump; and you will fly. This feeling is one that you will yearn to experience again, and again, and again.

> **"For once you have tasted flight, you will walk the earth with your eyes turned skywards, for there you have been and there you will long to return."**
> **~John H. Secondari**

Your perspective coupled with intentional action is the foundation that will force darkness to submit to light. It will be challenging at times, and you may want to give up, but if I can grow up and become a world record holder in an event that I've never seen before with my own two eyes, just imagine what you can do! My adversity in life has propelled me to be the long jump champion of the world, and it is now time for you to become a champion in an area that matters to you. Lace up your shoes, step to the line, and put on the blindfold!

Are you frightened? I hope you are. You are going to run, jump, and fly. You are facing Fear, but believe in your heart that you will succeed. Let us journey on now. This is Fear Sherpa.

~Lex Gillette, Special Olympic Gold Medalist and World Record Holder in the Long Jump and Triple Jump.

Contents

AVALANCHE

ONE

This is My Gift to You

This book has found you exactly at the right time in your life. The very fact that you are reading this is how I found meaning to the darkest and most soul crushing avalanche of my life... I was searching for you to gift this insight. As you read on, you will learn of this journey and it's my intent to guide you. It's how I changed suffering into these distilled lessons from my failures.

This is a remarkable perspective on harnessing Fear. I address Fear "in the moment," and "long-term," alike. From a long career in the U.S. Navy, I definitely knew Fear in-the-moment. However, I had to learn how to deal with the long-term types of Fear as well. Mine were being thought of as an impostor in the Navy Special Operations Community and not being good enough. If you struggle with these things, you too can learn to master them.

Our friend Fear is the gate-keeper to success, freedom and bliss. Everything we want is on the other side of our unique Fear. Left unchecked, Fear is the enforcer of our shame, and dictator of scarcity, causing us to be slaves of Fear. In this book, we will play with Fear and learn to transform this energy and turn it into a superpower.

Once I was rescued from a very dark place, a place where I forgot how to believe in myself and thought I was the failure. Because I decided to document this journey back to the land of the light, I wanted to be worthy of this suffering. The meaning I found has everything to do with you and serving as your guide on your journey to freedom that embracing our Fear can forge. I learned that it takes a team to rescue someone from a mountain avalanche. The same is true of our Fear, shame and guilt. Because an amazing rescuer once helped me to dig out, I desire to return the service to others. It is my hope that you decide to do the same with your deepest and darkest struggles. It is the fuel that forges us into the people we are called to be and the path to realizing our greatest self.

As you read on, you'll see the dark place that would become the birthplace of Fear Sherpa and later, spark the movement allowing this tribe to live extraordinary lives, enjoy outrageous dreams, and truly thrive again. This whole journey is that of the phoenix rising from the ashes of what was my greatest failure, and the costliest lessons learned in my life thus far. Before we dive in, it's amazing how God or the Universe is always acting on our behalf...always.

There's an amazing scene from the movie, *Concussion,* that moved me to the point of tears. This movie is the story of a very accomplished doctor, not familiar with the NFL and football in the U.S., who discovers the mental health issues the sport inflicts on its players. Watching this movie on a plane was the first real time that I can remember knowing that even with this broken past where I stopped believing in myself, that I survived the suffering in order to do something meaningful. In that moment, I wept. I was beginning to heal because my pain was finding its purpose and meaning.

In the movie, player Mike Webster goes mad and nobody asks why. They make fun of him. And now they want to pretend that disease doesn't exist. Dr. Omalu says, "They want to bury me. It's offensive. I'm offended. I'm the wrong person to have discovered that..."

His wife says: "There is no coincidence in this world. Tell me what's the statistical probability that you, not just a doctor, but

Bennet Omalu, come to America and end up here for you alone are the one to see this. Omalu (the name) means 'If you know you must come forth and speak.'"

What are the chances that a man strong enough to be a Navy Diver, yet smart enough to be a Bomb Technician, has the courage to suffer and the heart to want to teach others how to get back to freedom and light? The chances are zero. He chose me for His work.

> **"Don't turn away. Keep your gaze on the bandaged place. That's where the light enters you." ~Rumi**

This is my scar and it was here that the light entered. I hope you decide to master your Fear because once the light starts to radiate from your scar, the pain finds its meaning. Be worthy of this suffering because there is bliss on the other side.

TWO

Why You Need This Guide Book

Right now, Fear is the most abundant free drug in your world today. Because unchecked, Fear will steal your freedom and your abundant, happy life.

You'll blame fate, but you'll be wrong because truly it was Fear lurking in your subconscious that did the stealing.

You have the right to defend your mind and self from the effects of this prevalent drug.

Because Fear exists mostly in the subconscious level of our minds, lurking, making decisions without our consent. This process can slowly erode our freedoms, and our world becomes very small.

Although in the moment, under stress, while my world slows down and I'm the guy you want next to you in a stressful environment, you should know Fear stole from me; I too am a victim of Fear.

Please learn from my mistakes and build upon these ideas.

Fear was always present to some degree in my Navy Special Operations career. Because as I learned it's okay to feel Fear; we all did.

"Just overcome your Fear" is a waste of a powerful driving force and spoken by someone in need of understanding of our friend, Fear.

Because Fear in the hands of a trained master becomes a superpower and Fear in the hands of the untrained can be deadly.

Because as we wrestle with Fear, we are forging our courage and pressing our limitations outward. This prepares us for the moments in our lives when running away from Fear isn't the best option.

Because as the founder of Fear Sherpa, I'm not fearless. That's okay. Some days I master the bull, other days I fail, and tomorrow I try again. Only next time I'm a bit wiser. We learn. We grow and climb closer to our aspirations.

Because without forging our courage muscle, how can we let others know, "I need your help, I'm hurting," if we are too afraid?

THREE

Expectations and Agreement

As we journey together, there are a few expectations and agreements that I would like to share with you. You may be discovering this guidebook as you are moving through a major life change, attempting a mission that is very scary, or addressing long-term challenges with your relationship with Fear. As you will read and learn, my job is to help you see these challenges as opportunities where we can change and transform. This transformation will yield greater insight, clarity, and opportunity to live your best life. I'm going to travel to a dark place for me, a place that I very vividly remember when I was not loving myself, was ashamed of myself, and felt that I was the failure. As a warrior who in the moment could harness his Fear, then became suddenly embarrassed that I didn't have long term Fear handled, I realized that no one had ever taught me how to have a healthy relationship with Fear.

If you are not currently battling a demon such as this, there are two additional reasons to spend time with this guidebook. First, you may know someone going through the darkest part of their life. This book will help with understanding their pain and struggle, and teach you how to show up for them. Second, I hope we can discuss and decide before you have a major life change or setback what your emergency plan will be. This gives us time and space to practice and know the response because in the moment the prep work makes all the difference. I'd like for this to be a guidebook you can reference if you need it.

As you continue on this journey, I invite you to change and channel your relationship with Fear and its minions of shame, guilt, procrastination, worry, doubt, terrible self-talk, and imagined horrible outcomes. I invite you to look at Fear as your new superpower, a powerful source of energy, focus and fuel that we can harness, if only we can do the work and tame this formerly unbridled beast.

Also, please know that I use the words God and Universe. A spiritual reliance is important in this journey. In many ways, our relationship with Fear can be an addictive loop, especially when working through shame and guilt. Surrendering and believing in a higher power is something I found to be super helpful. For me, God and my faith made the difference. If that's not something that serves you, that's okay. In your mind, please replace God with whatever higher power you believe.

FOUR

Introducing Our Friend, Fear

As we begin this journey together, I invite you to answer a few questions honestly about your relationship with Fear as it is now.

- How does Fear show up for you? Where in your body do you first notice it? The first step is to understand the current situation. Please shine the light inwards and honestly look at what's there.
- What's a little Fear you'd like to work on? Having an intention and goal will help transform you from awareness into working knowledge and habits.
- In one year from now, what do you want your relationship with Fear to be?

Congratulations on starting this meaningful and vitally useful work! I invite you turn the light inward and document your starting position. Jump over to www.yoursecretsuper powerbook.com and begin using your free resources.

As you dig in and do this work, you'll begin to distance yourself from the start of this journey. The higher the climb, the more distance accumulates from the starting point. Capturing the feelings of being buried alive will become more and more distant. Once Fear dominion is mastered, the conscious competence may be forgotten. This is the most valuable part to helping recover friends and family in their avalanche.

My hope for you is to be part of this Fear Sherpa Tribe. That means helping others on their journey. Documenting your start and sharing your start will help those you are leading back to safety. This intention of wanting to help others on their path is always a great way to find meaning in doing deep and sometimes uncomfortable work.

How can this set back teach me more about myself? How can it serve me?

This changes the victim mentality, and helps us find some gratitude for the discomfort. I know it's challenging in the moment to see the value in it, but in retrospect, it's truly amazing to see how all these events come together to serve us.

"Those who have a 'why' to live, can bear with almost any 'how'." ~Viktor E. Frankl

As with the start of weight loss program, documenting the start is the "before" picture. Everything you do from here contributes to the "after" picture. In the future-casting portion of this work, we will explore using the imagination and language to manifest an incredible summit. The summit is the paradise of what our lives will be when Fear serves our needs, instead of us painfully serving Fear as our master.

FIVE

Hire Fear, Do It Now, and Make This Powerful Ally Work on Your Behalf

Today is a momentous day. Mark the date on your calendar because today we are putting Fear to work for us. What I've come to know is that we are the CEOs of our lives. It's appropriate to do some hiring today!

Dear Fear,

Thank you for serving me all these years. I apologize to you that I misunderstood your role and where your skills are best suited. I allowed you to run amuck and to steal things from me because you thought that it was keeping me safe. Because of my misunderstanding in our relationship, I didn't know that I needed to take a leadership role in managing such a powerful ally. You stepped up to protect us when I didn't.

It's my turn to take command. I have the conn, Fear; you are relieved.

I value your input as you are a trusted advisor. You're my coach; you help me see what's most important, and today I'm blessed to decide which course this ship goes. My life is going in a different direc-

tion. I'd like to build courage and trust discomfort as my teacher on my path to growth and realizing my fullest potential and mission. I still need you, but in a different role.

"A ship in harbor is safe, but that is not what ships are built for." ~John Shedd

Fear, please understand my life is meaningful and in order to affect my world and the world around me, I choose to be uncomfortable, for the bliss, truth and exhilaration on the other side of my nervousness, anxiety, and worry. I choose to listen to you in times of terror because I know you'll save my life and guide me to safety.

When it comes to worry, that has never been your area of expertise. I choose today to put my language, imagination, and mind into attracting what I truly desire, which is my life's purpose. I will stop using my imagination and language to create tragedies that aren't real. If I confused worry for terror, which feels the same, I cannot give you the attention you deserve in emergencies. I choose to use my language to articulate what I want, not what I'm trying to avoid. I will now use my imagination to work through the kinks, which is an area I'm trusting you with, but please know I will use my powers of visualization to attract and practice the outcomes I would like as opposed to the old way of visualizing the worst possible outcome.

With these practices, I seek dominion of my mind. I get to change my beliefs, which changes the way I see the world and the story I use to explain events. As a careful curator of language and thought, I'm prioritizing you for your true mission and purpose, which is to guide me through moments of terror and show me where the danger lies. I no longer ask or need you to be ever present, only appear during times of danger.

SIX

Naming Your Fear - We Are Not Our Fear

In this book, I use the word Fear as a proper noun. My intention with this is to denote the separation between our ego and our higher self. The ego tries to keep us safe, small, and comfortable. This is not a path to the life that we truly desire. Here the Fear (and other resistances) acts as the judicial arm of the ego that delivers discomfort for stepping outside of the well-worn and known path. If only we can change the story about what this feeling of resistance is, we can then learn to look at resistance as us growing. We are not our thoughts; we are not our Fear. We can take command if we choose to and the first step is naming our Fear.

Think of a name that you'll now call your servant Fear. He works for you now.

My Fear's name is Joe. He's learned over the years that he works for me. I value him but sometimes he can be a real asshole. Sometimes he waits until I'm tired, cold, hungry, alone, and frustrated to speak unkindly to me and tries to create self-doubt. He doesn't wait until I'm well-fed, happy, and in flow. He seems to wait until I'm vulnerable.

I like the name Joe because I don't believe Fear to be a malicious thing. He is just misunderstood. The most outrageous name one of my clients has given Fear is Maleficent, Walt Disney's Sleeping Beauty villain, the evil fairy and self-proclaimed "Mistress of All Evil." Maybe she's going a bit too far, but you get the point.

By naming our Fear, we gain further alignment for the proper order of things. Fear is a terrible master and makes an excellent servant. But with Fear, as with any powerful asset, we must step into our responsibility and leadership role.

The call to action for you in continuing this journey is deciding to be the master of Fear. Get to know your servant Fear and finally put Fear to work for you. Find your worksheet for your commitment to lead Fear at www.yoursecretsuperpowerbook.com. Sign, date and share your worksheet with others as this is a record of when you hired Fear to serve you.

Fear wears many masks:

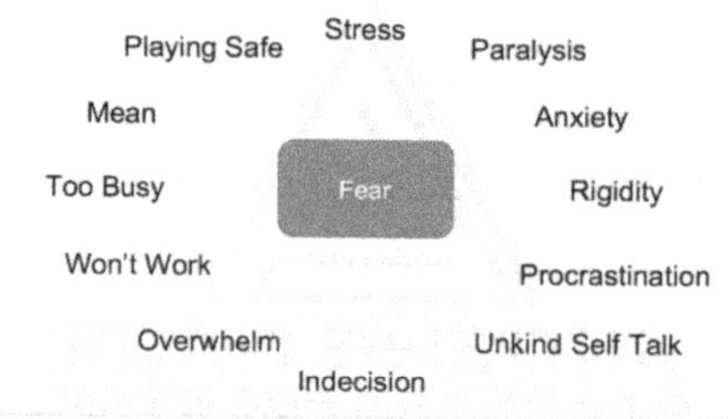

The secret to fighting your biggest Fear is actually not to overcome your Fear, but to learn to harness it. Fear is a powerful emotion that requires a master to be harnessed. You are learning to be that master right now by doing this life-changing work. Overcoming Fear will get you killed. Becoming Fear, and getting to know it is the key to thriving.

Learn to transform your Fear into your best friend, becoming a student of Fear, and use this powerful emotion to your advantage. Use your friend, Fear, to propel you to new heights.

The book you are holding is proof that anyone can learn this amazing skill of harnessing Fear. Thank you for your courage in deciding to take this upward climb with me on harnessing Fear. As a Former Navy Bomb Technician, I would like to be your guide. We are traveling to some dark places, but please stick with me; your own treasure is waiting for you in these scars and in the darkness. In fact, everything you truly want is on the other side of this work. Climb away!

> ***"This is how they survive. You must know this. You're too smart not to know this. They paint the world full of shadows... and then tell their children to stay close to the light. Their light. Their reasons, their judgments. Because in the darkness, there be dragons. But it isn't true. We can prove that it isn't true. In the dark, there is discovery, there is possibility, there is freedom in the dark once someone has illuminated it. And who has been so close to doing it as we are right now?" ~Captain Flint, "Black Sails"***

Peer into the darkness, and get to know it. Your treasure is waiting for you there in the shadows.

SEVEN

Birth of The Fear Sherpa

"Fear in the hands of a master becomes a superpower...Fear in the hands of the untrained can be deadly." ~Fear Sherpa

This guidebook that you hold in front of you is the product of years of work. It is the result of digging out of my avalanche, coming back from the greatest heartbreak of my life. I was fired from what I thought was my dream job. That dream job was being selected as a Special Operations Commander in the U.S. Navy EOD (Explosive Ordnance Disposal, Navy Bomb Technician). This avalanche led me to find my actual dream, which is leading the Fear Sherpa Movement.

In college, my greatest desire was to be a Navy EOD Officer. Bomb Techs...Imagine the movie *The Hurt Locker* but cooler. When I was in college, I spent two weeks with a special unit in Virginia Beach. We jumped out of helicopters and blew shit up. I was amazed at how physically demanding it was just to get to the problems we were tasked with and how cerebrally challenging these problems we solved as a team were. I was hooked. I knew this was what I was going to do in the Navy.

Returning home from that trip, I went to church and lit every single candle. I begged God to please help me to become a Navy EOD Tech. I strategized with my coaches, studied hard, and did the work. I was selected as one of seventeen ROTC officers that year to start the program.

I'll never forget the day that my class advisor called me to tell me the good news. Our whole class was eagerly awaiting notification of which community would select us to serve our country. I needed my class advisor to repeat three times that I was selected. To say that I was excited was an understatement. The next morning, at our unit's morning physical training, I can't remember a time when I was so fired up. I couldn't help but motivate my classmates because I was going somewhere special.

During the first half of my career, I couldn't believe I was getting paid to do what I was doing. I spent an entire month in San Diego with fellow EOD and SEAL Operators learning how use skydiving as a fun way to commute to work. We blew up cars on the demolition range. We went to some of the best shooting schools in the world, and learned some really interesting skills. I gladly would have exchanged tens of thousands of dollars to learn and do these things.

It taught me to look at the world differently. We get to change our environments to reduce danger and increase the chances of our success. I remember also being an advisor for the secret service for missions all over the world for some really important people. My professional opinion mattered and I felt like James Bond. And God, I loved my men and feeling part of this winners' circle.

I was living my dream job. People would ask me what I did for a living. I was so proud to tell them, "I'm a Special Operations Officer in the U.S. Navy." It was the reason I got out of bed in the morning. To be a better officer, to be stronger, smarter and to be a better leader were my North Star. Plus, it was damn cool!

My career was going great, until I started messing up. I didn't do anything nor did any single event preclude me from continuing on my path. That path I so desired was to be selected to DEVGRU (SEAL TEAM 6) or as we called them, "The Jedi's." That wasn't in the cards. It was the death of 1,000 cuts and it all stemmed from my Fear. In the moment when I was jumping out of airplanes, working on improvised explosive devices, or shooting, my world slowed down during the extreme moments life offers. My body goes into a flow state where I perform at my best. The Fear I was unprepared to deal with, however, is the long-term systemic Fear. The Fear of being found out an impostor. I didn't believe I really deserved my spot in this Special Operations career, which was insane. But, for whatever reason, I didn't believe I was worthy of the pin and uniform I actually earned. I lived in Fear that my community would think I wasn't part of the brotherhood. This is crazy to hear myself read this out loud. After all, I was hand-picked, did well at Dive School, and then completed one of the most challenging training pipelines in the military, EOD school. Sitting at the table with these battle-hardened warriors, I was honored and yet still believed I had tricked everyone on the selection committee. There was a seasoned officer who believed in me and I found myself not taking full advantage of his mentorship because I was afraid to show the areas where I was weak. In confrontations, in defending my decisions, I let people treat me like I was lucky to be there. For our mission with the Rangers, my command was afraid that I would get eaten alive because of this. Also, I was too afraid of looking weak. I didn't have the courage to say, "Sir, the mission you have selected me for is unwinnable as a new, junior officer without his senior enlisted advisor. Please give me something more manageable."

What I learned later was that this individual was using this event to show the world that I was an unworthy member of the EOD community. Never before was I targeted this way. I had no idea how to respond to such an inner threat. My demise had a lot to do with me being afraid of being found out as an impostor and lacking the courage to say "no" to dangerous situations.

I was reassigned from the position of platoon commander of the men I loved and would have done anything to protect, and relegated to the Night Watch Captain. I failed. My unit saw me miss the target and wanted nothing to do with me, or at least that's I what I believed. I'm not sure if I excluded myself from these warriors, but I felt alone. I felt like I had leprosy and no one wanted to be around me for fear of catching this infection that I possessed.

I'm grateful for the CrossFit gym and community that became my refuge. I took pleasure in the workouts and defeating the guys that made my life harder. I read *Born to Run: A Hidden Tribe, Superathletes, and the Greatest Race the World Has Never Seen* by Christopher McDougall, and fell in love with barefoot running. I began training for a marathon.

But it was the unconditional love of my Mom and Dad, my beautiful wife, and time celebrating the mass at Chapel that gave me some relief in this terribly dark time. There was also a young sailor, Thor, who needed my mentorship. These things gave me purpose. To this day, every time I use Skype, I'm reminded of when I was a half a world away, longing to be in the same place as my loved ones on the other side of the world.

It was miraculous how I was selected for this community. In a way, it was miraculous the way I was picked from the fray as well. I really do believe God had a plan for me. At the time that my career began crumbling, the nightmares of the metal box with the flag draped over it became a recurring nightmare. This I used as motivation to train harder.

Thank God I didn't get what I thought I wanted. If I was allowed to deploy to Afghanistan to support Army Special Forces, I would be a different person. Maybe I would be here, but maybe not. This wrestling with my Fear, shame, and guilt forged me into the leader of Fear Sherpa that I am today. I'm glad for that. Never would I want to walk that path again or wish it on others, but great turmoil is the forge that molds us into our greatest self.

I'll never forget the day that my life changed forever with two lines of dialogue. The Commanding Officer called me into his office for a meeting during our team training as we were gearing up to deploy to Afghanistan. This was a leader I still respect to this day. He taught me a great deal. I knew exactly what this conversation was going to cover.

He said, "Brian, I have lost a lot of sleep over this, but you are not the man to lead your team in Afghanistan."

My heart fell through my chest and it was the single greatest heartbreak I'd ever felt. I was out of time to have a completed combat deployment to qualify as an EOD Officer. So, I didn't have to the leave the Navy, but I did have to leave the community. He was very supportive in the coming months and I learned later that he was a big reason I got a second chance after failing in Iraq eighteen months before that. Leaving that meeting, I went to see my men for what would be the last time as their leader. I said, "You have taught me a lot, I hope I have taught you something. It was my greatest professional honor to lead you. Take care of each other and come home safe."

I retreated to my little office where I wept tears of shame and failure. I had never experienced heartbreak like that. In all of the effort and sacrifice, I had never given myself so completely to something. To hear you're not good enough, that my best wasn't good enough, shattered me. He didn't say, "Not good enough," but that's what I heard.

Shrek, one of my team leaders, hugged me and told me that I was a good officer. It meant a lot. And just as my time in EOD started, it was over. I finished my time as the Training Officer of the Diving Command, MDSU 2. I enjoyed it and learned that I was in fact a good officer.

It was time for other things and that is how Fear Sherpa was born. I started working with a very talented coach. She would become a dear friend, my Jewish Auntie. She had me read Viktor Frankl's, *Man's Search for Meaning.*

In the book, when Frankl was a prisoner in a concentration camp, he found ways of finding freedom in the most austere and disgusting of situations. He learned that in the space between the stimulus of the terrible things that happen to us and the reaction to these things, our freedom exists. It sometimes is the only freedom we have, the freedom to choose our reaction. When the guards would withhold food, Frankl would decide, "Today is the day I'm starting my fast."

Other times, he would give what little food he had to the other prisoners. In those decisions, in the most horrific of circumstances, Frankl found freedom.

He also spoke about being worthy of one's suffering. "...[B]ut there was no need to be ashamed of tears. For tears bore witness that a man had the greatest of courage, the courage to suffer."

After reading his book, I decided to be worthy of my suffering as well. If Frankl could find meaning in the Holocaust, surely I could find meaning and be worthy of the pain I felt through losing what I thought to be my dream job. The heartbreak, the guilt, and the shame could be meaningful if I could help others through similar difficult times. It didn't make sense. Yet, while I felt alone and struggled in Iraq, I didn't know the path I would choose when I learned EOD was no longer my home or my identity. I didn't know that God had a different plan for me, one in which I would help people, the same way my amazing friend and coach helped me. I decided to write about my scar and be courageous enough to spend time with it. I knew this would be valuable for others, because self-rescue in these situations isn't possible. We need the help of others to dig us out from life's avalanches. I decided to write out a road map to help others through obstacles and recover from being slaves of Fear.

I kept a red Moleskine journal and documented the treasure I discovered in my fresh scar. I brought back insights about Fear and shame from spending time with this darkness. This would prove to be my roadmap to digging back out to finding the light again. Those pages contain what I just shared about my last day as an EOD commander, future-casting for what I desired my life to be, and how I wanted to help others through difficult times. On the last page of that journal, I wrote a thank you note to this valuable piece of survival gear. As this journal opened its pages to me, I discovered more about myself. It allowed me to dream again and know that I could help others survive. It also provided a log of the altitude I have gained since my avalanche. I knew this documented journey would be valuable to others as they wrestled with their darkness. This journal is my prized possession. It's how this guidebook and movement was born. Because you are reading this guide, you've helped me find meaning in the suffering I endured. Thank you for being part of this amazing transformation. Like the tale of the phoenix, rising from the ashes of failure, shame and Fear, this journal has transformed life into something more beautiful than I could have imagined.

To My Trusted Red Confidant and Teacher,

Thank you, Red Moleskine Journal, for opening yourself as I opened myself. You were my guide in surviving my avalanche and the loss of what I thought was my dream job. You helped me realize that God's plan for me was much bigger than the mission I thought I was destined to walk as a Special Operations Officer in the United States Navy.

Your pages allowed me the space to dream and to memorialize the often-difficult digging and climbing out of my avalanche. You allowed me to have hope and discover a method of helping others improve their relationships to our friend and companion, Fear. The tears shed on your pages allowed me to see the beauty of what these darker emotions give us. They serve as the changing winds and the warning that our lives are forever different now.

The gift you gave is this beautiful pause followed by a space where different decisions manifest because of this life-changing explosion. It is this disruption from the easy and comfortable life that we once had. There is treasure in this scar inflicted that I discovered by gazing back on your pages. You helped me see the progress that I have made since the Navy told me we didn't need you to do your bit (NOT in laying my life down for my men, for my nation and fellow countrymen. You helped me see the decision I made to be a guide after they [the Navy] granted me my freedom and I chose to lead this movement.)

Thank you for the magic contained in future-casting that we did together. I now see the miracles that are coming into reality. You let me share them with you. I'm lucky to have amazing people that helped me dig out, but you helped me write a map and directions to the light, freedom, abundance, and outrageous dreaming again. You are a part of the reason I feel like a warrior again. You were part of my vital survival gear. The information your pages contain will help other avalanche survivors.

I appreciate you, Red Journal. The Fear Sherpa mission would not have been possible without you. Thank you for your service. It's time for the next act where we teach others what you contain and help them climb towards something even better than we can possibly imagine.

Peace and blessings,

Brian J. Muka
Fear Sherpa
December 22, 2016

You will gain insights and tools to work with in the following pages and start to harness your Fear. I hope for you that Fear can become a dear friend. It takes work to tame this wild bull that is our friend, Fear. I promise the work you do will be worth it, if you are courageous enough to push against this powerful and very misunderstood driving force.

As I started writing, I realized we have a choice. Either you are the master of your Fear or Fear masters you and can steal everything. The truth and secret are, we have always had this choice, but Fear lurks and operates in the subconscious. We are going to turn the light inwards and begin working on this important relationship with Fear. Fear can steal from you, make decisions without your consent, and rob you of an otherwise abundant life.

After my fall from Navy EOD, a warrior who helped establish the original Seal Teams offered me a training manager position in Dubai. It was killer money, life-changing money, and would have extended my James Bond lifestyle. Fear said "No" on my behalf. I told people that I was worried about my safety, and that the U.S. Cavalry wouldn't be there to rescue me if I needed them. I declined a quarter million dollars a year with another US $50,000 for living expenses. I would have come home with a beautiful sailing yacht that would be my home while over there. In reality, I was terrified of failing again. I lost my confidence to be a combat leader and Fear stole this amazing opportunity from me without my actual consent.

It took me a long time to dig out from that. There were a lot of amazing opportunities after the Navy which I rejected because of this Fear.

I remember when my Jewish Auntie asked me, "Do you believe that God loves you unconditionally?"

I said, "Yes, and I know this is true."

She asked, "Do you love you unconditionally?"

I struggled to answer and finally replied, "No, I don't."

This was the first moment that I realized that I needed to learn to love myself. I was so embarrassed and ashamed to admit that to another human, especially someone I respected so much.

This book is the roadmap I used to change that last statement and I hope it proves valuable to your journey back to the land where it's okay to love yourself, dream huge, live abundantly, and do scary stuff
.

Have fun improving your relationship with our friend, Fear. Now, let's play and have some fun with this!

Summary of Avalanche

1. Fear is a powerful and misunderstood force that requires a master. Left unbridled it can get us killed; harnessed Fear becomes a potent superpower. We get to choose and become that master!
2. Our greatest setbacks provide the greatest opportunity for growth, if only we seek the learning opportunity. We cannot see it in the moment, but with courage and faith, we can decide to be better as a result of these avalanches. Remember, setbacks and discomforts are not punishments. They are the path and the opportunity for our growth, true bliss, and exhilaration.
3. Fear is a potent source of fuel and focus. We must become its commander or Fear loses its effectiveness to get us to safety and see the true danger versus the imagined worry and doubt. Decide to be Fear's master and thrive.
4. Suffering is never in vain if we can find meaning. The same is true for discomfort. What is this setback trying to teach me? Who can I help with my climb back to the

light? These answers will lead us to the biggest versions of ourselves.

BASE CAMP

EIGHT

Assemble Your Rescue Team and Make a Plan

The phrase, "I'm good, I don't need your help!" is a great way to get yourself killed if you find yourself buried alive in any avalanche. If you were to become buried alive in a physical avalanche under thousands of tons of snow and ice, it's an unrealistic expectation to think you can to save yourself without a team. So why then do we expect ourselves to be able to self-rescue for life's emotional avalanches?

In many ways, the emotional avalanche is more challenging because it's not something for which we are well practiced. This is very serious because suicide is a major challenge to our warrior communities. As a result, a major motivator for me, especially with my work with veterans, is to prevent suicide. With that said, using the tools and information in this section is worth your time. I urge you to plan now. It could save you or help you to truly live again.

When is the best time to write the emergency plan? The answer is **before you find yourself in the emergency.**

Who will be on your team? Here are some key words to inspire creating the most robust team possible:

1. Family members you trust implicitly.

2. Your "ride or die" friends (ride it out or die trying, precious people to be blessed with).

3. A professional. This can include a therapist, coach, doctor, etc. (I cannot recommend this more).

4. Support group.

5. Mastermind/Men's or women's group.

6. People in your faith community.

7. People with whom you work out that you trust.

As you engage with this work, our team will get us very far. For stretches of time, it's completely okay to have our team give us a breather. But also know also that it's unrealistic to think that you will be pulled 100% by the work of others. They have their own water to carry. And when we have built our strength and reserves, we can return the favor.

The adventure to which I'm inviting you requires you to actually walk through life's scary doors to the other side of Fear. No one can actually take these steps for us. You will do it and hopefully have your tribe's love and support to cross this seemingly dark valley. Remember it is in the darkness that discovery happens. It's also where we learn true freedom and realize our greatest potential.

I want you to develop a journaling practice. Be sure to obtain *Your Secret Superpower Daily Journal: 100 Days to Tame Your Fear.* Please don't buy another journal that will sit on your shelf. Decide to commit to a writing practice. Your deepest insights, release from trauma, and a space to record your wins (altitude gained) are waiting for your words.

I've been committed to this journaling practice for over eight years now and it has been one of the best gifts to myself. By flipping through my words from the past, I can remember where I was, what I was learning, insights, and great quotes. My favorite part is seeing how things have come together by turning my dreams into goals through writing them into reality. That's the result.

In their book, *Opening Up by Writing It Down, Third Edition: How Expressive Writing Improves Health and Eases Emotional Pain,* authors James W. Pennebaker and Joshua M. Smyth explain that through writing, we can ease a significant amount of our own traumas. Give this a read and do the exercises.

Later on in this book, we will talk in depth about interruption techniques for when the self-doubt, worry, shame, guilt or any of the other of Fear's minions seek to usurp command from you. I'd recommend picking three "go to" pattern interrupts. For me, my three are:

1. Breath work, especially with my crew.

2. Playing and singing on my ukulele, especially for the enjoyment of others.

3. Depending on what I need in the moment, a hard workout or time writing in the journal.

In the keynotes I deliver, a mantra I share is:

- Breathe, gain control of physiology.
- Smile, turn nervousness into excitement.
- Gratitude for the current opportunity to expand.

When the intensity is higher than can be shouldered alone, my buddy Dave and I will don our weight vests, look forward, and move together by walking. While walking, we will share what feels overwhelming. Whatever the challenge was at the start, it's always better at the end of those walks. My point is have a plan ready and an accountability partner.

In the next chapter we will start talking about the inner adventure and the power of our thoughts.

NINE

The Inner Adventure and Our Thoughts - Do Your Inner Monologue and Imagination Serve You?

Thought yields great power. The physical manifestation of everything we can see is the effect of thought. Everything started as a thought. And I want you to know that "seeing is believing" is the biggest lie that there is.

Why? If you're waiting to see it to believe it, you are waiting on a lie. Because if we see and don't believe we logically explain anything to the contrary to this belief. That is the reason miracle cures are explained away by the medical science lens of what is known.

Our well-curated thoughts and language become the seeds that lead to change, progress, and creation. We must exercise caution and care when curating our language. The words and thoughts we use don't describe our world. They create it.

Finally, true belief is action. In the words of Peter Drucker, "Tell me what you value and I might believe you. Show me your calendar and your bank statement and I'll show you what you really value." Awareness of how we are spending our resources is important for accountability, our growth, and the realization of dreams.

So, knowing this we are called to a great responsibility and strive towards love while embracing Fear as the gatekeeper and teacher.

Fear protects the love, bliss, abundance, and universal intelligence, and it is reserved for those willing to do the work challenge through the unknown and uncomfortable. There are these mini deaths along the way. They are:

- Death of a dream.
- Death of a relationship.
- The end of a dream job.
- Catastrophic medical injury.
- Losing capacity due to age.

There are some we have already experienced:

- Birth and leaving the comfort and safety of the womb.
- Separating from our mother, a loss of oneness.
- Leaving the purity of being a newborn as we're socialized to believe we aren't enough.
- Loss of our innocence and believing life is hard and expecting hardship. "No Pain, No Gain."

In all of these things, we must pass through the Fear of the unknown. The Fear also begins updating the map that we used to believe was our truth and lens. In order to actualize what we really want we must have the courage to update the outdated map. It is a requirement. In a way the ego suffers a death, as the update means the previous model was wrong. The process of updating the map is often times uncomfortable and exhausting.

In terms of navigating the path to attain our desires, using the most accurate map will make arriving at our destination possible. When plotting a course using an outdated map many hazards aren't yet charted and even the bearing to our destination could be wrong. The cost is deep work and the reward is actually hitting our target. Without regularly updating our map we get lost and end up crashing on the rocks of life.

If I possess faith in my belief it must cause action. Without belief I cannot take bold courageous action. Belief without action is worthless until it inspires action.

A belief that I carry is the law of relativity as a universal law. It states that hardship isn't a test. If we can change our belief that hardship actually is the way we become the person we were meant to, it becomes a teacher. The major advantage is changing your belief takes away suffering and pain. I know that during my workouts, I don't wallow in the dread of a challenging sprint to CrossFit workouts. I look forward to them and am grateful for the training stimulus. What if we can view life's challenges as opportunities? They become the path to achieving our dreams. What a better story!

"The journey of a thousand miles begins with a single step." ~Lao Tzu

TEN

Fear of Our Success and Power

"Our deepest Fear is not that we are inadequate. Our deepest Fear is that we are powerful beyond measure. It is our light, not our darkness that most frightens us. We ask ourselves, Who am I to be brilliant, gorgeous, talented, fabulous? Actually, who are you *not* to be? You are a child of God. Your playing small does not serve the world. There's nothing enlightened about shrinking so that other people won't feel insecure around you. We are all meant to shine, as children do. We were born to make manifest the glory of God that is within us. It's not just in some of us; it's in everyone. And as we let our own light shine, we unconsciously give other people permission to do the same. As we're liberated from our own Fear, our presence automatically liberates others." ~Marianne Williamson

I want to address this early in your development. As you continue to make progress in taming Fear and gaining altitude from your avalanche, there's a Fear that we need to address. It's the Fear of success and the Fear of how powerful we are becoming.

The old story of us not being successful enough or having no power is like a warm familiar blanket. Even more dangerous is that you probably know and interact with many people who share this belief as well. There will be a transition period when the old story and the old friends and associates won't be a fit anymore and the new story and people haven't 100% materialized just yet. Left unchecked we humans typically will revert back to the path of least resistance, especially because many people are unwilling to do this deep work to obtain freedom from the tyranny of Fear. I do believe that they have the best of intentions, but your journey feels unsafe to them and they want to keep you safe and comfortable (remember, comfort is the enemy). They don't know any better. As they see you stepping into your power and seeing more success, these people will feel more and more uncomfortable and may try talking to you or guilting you back into your old ways. Stay strong.

The internal struggle:

- Who am I to be ...
- I'm just a ....
- What if I fail?
- Impostor syndrome, "What if I'm not good enough?"

Answers:

- What if I'm exactly what's needed?
- Doesn't matter who I was; It's who I am now.
- What if I succeed?
- What if I am good enough?

Our language and our preparation for the self-doubt is important.

Our conditioning and ego want us to stay small, safe, and comfortable. The above questions bring out the smallness in us. The second set of questions brings out the biggest and boldest versions of ourselves. This is exactly what is needed in our tribe and in our world. People need to be prepared to be unreasonable.

> **"The reasonable man adapts himself to the world. The unreasonable man persists in trying to adapt the world to himself. Therefore, all progress depends on the unreasonable man." ~George Bernard Shaw**

Take Mohammad Ali for example. For many years, he called himself great. He had his camp call him great. He did this because he wanted to believe it. After all the repetition he eventually brought this into his consciousness and truly believed in his greatness. Now when history looks back at this man, he is known as the greatest of all time.

How does your inner voice serve or enslave you? Does it inspire you to be great or does it discourage your greatness?

The same thing is true about the lie.

> **"It is easier to believe a lie that one has heard a thousand times than to believe a fact that one has never heard before." ~Robert Lynd**

So be suspect of people's opinions, but especially your own, the one we hear in the inner monologue. As you begin to notice the frequent stories we tell ourselves, ask, Does this story make hitting our goals easier or harder? What if the thought "I'm not good enough" is the lie repeated a thousand times? The imposter syndrome is so common, a title for it was coined. This means that many of us, myself included, kept ourselves from the realization of our greatest selves and lives.

Knowing this, my high school and college experiences would

have been very different. There were beautiful women interested in me, but I didn't believe it. The lie I told myself was, "How could they be into me?" I would eventually find a way to make my belief a reality and mess up the relationship in some way.

Self-sabotage is something that with your mindfulness and writing practices, you can identify and use to make different decisions. Remember, "seeing is believing" is a lie that we have heard a thousand times. What we believe is the filter we apply and consequently experience.

Thoughts repeated enough become beliefs. The beliefs that we hold affect what we see, notice, and feel. Make sure your beliefs are true and serve your mission. "True and useful" is the goal.

When you believe it and repeat it enough, it becomes true. We must be impeccable curators of our language and observers of our thoughts.

ELEVEN

Prep the Battlefield

You may have just lost a loved one, experienced a terrible injury resulting in the loss of a limb or physical ability, received a diagnosis of a terrible illness, or lost your dream. These events can serve as a wakeup call when you are ready.

It was for me.

In Buddhism there is the something called Samsara, which is the etching of our record of life, the deep groove created by our habits. Wake up, eat breakfast, work, workout, eat dinner, relax, and then do it over and over and over again. How does this etching affect you, your life, your loved ones, and your mission? In this loop, we have a life that is "good enough". This is the kiss of death.

There is a gift here that avalanches provide. As firefighters fight oil-well fires, they use an explosive to create a temporary vacuum to stop the flames for a moment and cap the well. These avalanches, these explosions, can disrupt the Samsara, the deeply etched grooves of "good enough" lives.

In the book *Good to Great: Why Some Companies Make the Leap...and Others Don't,* author Jim Collins teaches that the enemy of great is good. Very few people will leap from the good life, through the valley, until the great life is reached. It's these avalanches that provide the pause and interruption of Samskara to take our lives from mundane to the extraordinary.

I'm repeating this on purpose. This is one of the **most expensive lessons I have ever learned:**

> **"Every adversity, every failure, every heartbreak, carries with it the seed of an equal or greater benefit." ~Napoleon Hill, *Think and Grow Rich***

We must be on the lookout for these veiled opportunities for success or breakthroughs. I'm telling you all of this because there can be value in pain. I'm also telling you that there will be people in your life that do not have the depth of character to support you in dark times. They cannot. It's not because they don't want to, but they have not been through an avalanche for that compassion to be forged.

A friend of mine is stunningly beautiful, super successful, and struggled to find love and meaningful work. Her group of friends cannot be with her in this tough time because they have never failed. They never had this grief, this shame, this doubt to work through. And as this continues to come up, it becomes increasingly uncomfortable for the non-survivors to be with her, because they have not suffered in this way.

So, I ask you if you currently wear a "survivor" t-shirt of an avalanche, a death, a loss, a grieving, a mistake, a guilt, a shame, any of that. If so, please be on the lookout for other people going through the same thing.

We. Can. Help. Each. Other.

It will seem strange and serendipitous when you start opening your eyes and looking for other survivors, we are everywhere. It's crazy how we can identify each other. Let's build our family and tribe as a safe home for fellow survivors.

TWELVE

Look Inward: Find Your Own Answers

I'd like to show you how to give yourself a gift. I'd highly recommend documenting your process and progress. We touched on this briefly in Chapter 4.

Similar to a weight loss or other body-transformative journey, people often take "before" pictures at their heaviest or worst phase, to contrast and to prove their success. They will amaze themselves and others by documenting the total change. When the weight is lost, the shredded body manifests. Time to take "after" pictures. That's documenting the journey.

The videoing, the blogging, the writing - however you choose to spend time with your scar, this documentation will be valuable when you want to see how far you have climbed and also what it was like when the scar was fresh. As you climb, you forget what it was like in the very start of this journey. This can be a fantastic perspective and gift to others following your example if you want.

What I'd recommend is, decide and commit to the particular method you want to use as your log to track the altitude gained since your avalanche. The writing and documenting are nothing short of miraculous. The clarity and perspective shifts are valuable. This can be a way to help yourself heal. In mindfully writing, you access the special part of yourself.

I believe that God and the Universe connect to universal intelligence. It requires a quiet reflection, a type of meditation that connects to the fact that in some areas, you lack knowledge and/or experience. But you can tap into the Universal Collective Wisdom. The ideas from somewhere else flow through the pen or pencil. I promise you will be surprised at the answers you find if you only turn the light inward. Be courageous enough to look for unique insights and new directions.

The goals you wish to achieve, the objects you desire, the emotions you want to feel, the dream life for which you strive - put it in *Your Secret Superpower Daily Journal.* There's magic that happens when these ideas and desires enter the real world through the written or spoken word. It's crazy how these manifest.

I'm amazed at how the first few pages of my red Moleskine journal documented the last few minutes in front of my men in EOD Platoon 12-2-2. I wept. You can see the tear marks on the page. I'm glad I have these writings. This is my "before" picture, when I was broken, and no longer had my North Star to guide my life and decisions. And now looking back on that moment, there is so much altitude that I have gained from then. You too will survive and thrive after your avalanche.

A great gift to myself is my yearly review of the pages of my red journals. They remind me of:

1. How far I have climbed.
2. Seeing how pain has taught me.
3. The worry in crossing through scary doors. In every instance, without fail, resistance felt huge and soul crushing for the doors that really mattered. These were opportunities to expand greatly. Also, I built faith knowing the bliss on the other side is exhilarating. Self-confidence, joy, and freedom awaited me there. I promise

you, that every time it feels this scary, the truth and enlightenment stand ready for you on the other side, no matter what.

4. Gratitude for the challenges. In retrospect, they presented the best opportunities.
5. The Universe is working on my behalf.
6. Connecting the stars from what seemed like chaos and the pain associated with those transitions. It was this resistance that allowed my expansion so that I could truly living life to the fullest.
7. The courage it took me in every setback to get back up and try again. When I did, I conveyed a stronger and wiser version of me.

My prayer for you is to archive and release your own unique experience and gain altitude by leaps and bounds.

Here is an excerpt from the last page of my personal struggle. In writing in my journal, I made space to dream again. It allowed me to see the treasure that was hidden in the scar. The tools I have used, the steps taken, the guidebook you are holding right now all stemmed from my journaling. If you like this book, if you think others will want to read your story someday, make it easy and find your own insights and truths.

As I shared in Chapter 1, thirteenth-century poet Rumi, said:

"Don't turn away. Keep your gaze on the bandaged place. That's where the light enters you."

Once the light starts entering, you will not, you cannot go back. There's no putting the genie back in the bottle once that healing starts to happen. You start to find meaning from the suffering you survived. Because not everyone survives this. The things we are talking about are the Fear of being a failure, Fear of being an impostor, and the shame of feeling like you're the mistake or the guilt of something that you've done. Some people don't survive that. Most people going through that let it kill them in terms of killing their ability to dream and live life on their terms. It doesn't happen immediately. There's a grieving period. I pray that your grieving period, if you are living it right now, is short. Take the time you need to heal. But, don't let it keep you in this shame prison.

Summary of Base Camp

1. Fear is a powerful and misunderstood force that requires a master. We get to be that master!
2. Our greatest setbacks provide the greatest opportunity for growth. We cannot see it in the moment, but with courage and faith, we can decide to be better as a result of these avalanches.
3. Suffering is never in vain if we can find meaning. What is this setback trying to teach me? Who can I help with my climb back to the light? Remember it's not a punishment, but rather an opportunity to grow. The emotional discomfort is similar to the muscle pain after a workout that results in growth and adaption. The emotional pain is the same.
4. Keep a journal. One of the greatest gifts to myself is my continuous journals from my avalanche. This makes it easier to find joy in the climb by giving gratitude for the hard earned progress.

ICE

THIRTEEN

"Breathe, Mother F*#&er"

"In the Bhagavad Gita they say, 'The mind under control is your best friend, the mind wandering about is your worst enemy.' Make it your best friend, to the point where you can rely on it. Your mind makes you strong from within. It is your wise companion. The sacrifices you make will be rewarded. Life doesn't change, but your perception does. It's all about what you focus on. Withdraw from the world's influence and no longer be controlled by your emotions. If you can grab the wheel of your mind, you can steer the direction of where your life will go." ~ Wim Hof and Justin Rosales

So, you've heard my story and the birth of Fear Sherpa. It is my scar and it was here, that the light entered. It was in my red Moleskine journal where I spent time with this scar, the heartbreak, and the darkness that I carried. With courage, I spent time with this suffering and my search for meaning for it. Every time I went to the scar I came home with treasure. What you are actually reading and what you hold in your hands is the product of those trips to the scar and the treasure I unearthed. The first half of this tale is how Fear stole from me, without my permission.

I desire for you to gain control of your life again. We begin to take command of our lives and of our powerful ally, Fear, in the space between the stimulus and reaction. It is in this gap where freedom exists that we choose how to respond. It is not simply overcoming Fear, because this is a terrible waste of time and energy. Rather, how do we harness Fear? How can Fear be a gift? How does Fear turn into a superpower for those courageous enough to master it?

How can Fear be my teacher?

If you decide to keep reading you are going to find out. What follows next are the tactics of how we actually do this.

FOURTEEN

The Breath: Wim Hof and the Ice Bath Method

I'd like to introduce you to Wim Hof. He is a fellow avalanche survivor. His world crumbled when his wife took her own life.

He became a daredevil. He started doing crazy things underwater under the ice, and free climbing on rock faces. One day, he was completely paralyzed. He couldn't physically move his body, frozen. As he was stuck on the rock face, he started breathing.

After a few dozen breaths, he was able to move his arms again. A few dozen more in, he was able to move his legs. Through the breath he was able to start climbing again, and would ascend back to safety. This breathing brought him back to life. It can and will do the same for you if you let it.

One of the tools often utilized is the Wim Hof method. In the first part of the Wim Hof Method, we learn and practice breathing technology. We train the body to accept more oxygen through breathing deeply through the diaphragm 30 to 50 times. We are over-breathing, taking in more oxygen than usual. In the second half of the practice, we release the air in the lungs by easily blowing out and then resting with empty lungs as long as possible. This method is my favorite way to meditate and reset the brain and body.

In those moments between breaths, I can feel the change in how my heartbeats feel. The heartbeats change from a hard pounding to an easy flutter that is very slow and relaxing. I find calm, a safe center, even if in the midst of a hurricane.

The effects of this are enhanced by practicing with a group. I'm beginning to understand why monks meditate together. I notice an energy exchange that happens only when trust is built in the safety of a tribe. It is when groups are doing things in sync with each other that safety is found. My coach, Brandon Powell, calls it "the rhythm of life". Here are examples of the rhythm of life:

1. The beating of the heart.
2. Playing music in band or a group.
3. Singing with a church choir.

For our purposes, there exists some magic in the way the breath syncs with a group of people. It fosters a sense of intimacy, safety, and allows the body to fully let go of tension and Fear. This is why practicing the Wim Hof method with a lovely group of people is so effective.

We use drumming to sync the breathing of the whole group. We create a very safe space and, in this safe space we then can explore and go deeper to the nervous system to find peace and connection with others.

Also, in the Wim Hof Style of Breathing, we experience the benefit of hyperbaric medicine. There are some diseases that do not like oxygen and by breathing, we can change our body's chemistry into an enhanced environment where our body can thrive. Furthermore, we are able to explore what we know of the consciousness, the buzzing of the hands the tingling, and experiencing the roaring in the ears. It's all science - going deeper into the nervous system where we can actually clean the body. The Wim Hof Method concluded in peer-reviewed medical journal articles and experiments that man has dominion of the body through the mind and breath. Science did not know we had this control before Wim Hof made his discoveries. These insights are imbedded in each of us. We simply forgot. These superpowers are already here and they are yearning to be put into practice.

Please understand that it isn't just the oxygen, as CO2 plays a very important role in the body. Without CO2, we wouldn't be able to utilize oxygen. In the space between breaths we are changing from very basic (alkaline PH in the body, 7.8PH roughly) to acidic. It is the change between the basic to the acidic that we can actually train our cardiovascular systems. During the breath hold, the empty lung portion, CO2 will rise. With this build up, the effect of aerobic respiration, nitric oxide increases.

The 1998 Nobel Prize in Physiology or Medicine was awarded for discovering nitric oxide's role as a cardiovascular signaling molecule. We can use this molecule to expand the sinuses and lungs, thereby making breathing easier. I use a system from the Oxygen Advantage before bed to ease into sleep.

Please go to your references and watch this video on Oxygen Advantage: www.yoursecretsuperpowerbook.com. Please, if you love yourself, watch this video. It speaks to the reasons we must use our nose for breathing. Nose breathing produces more calm in the body and works in better harmony with the body as opposed to mouth breathing.

- *Mouth breathing only for panic purposes and eating.*
- *Nose breathing for all other breathing.*

If we are heavy sigh-breathing through the mouth, we are producing noradrenaline and the body must work harder. We are put into the fight or flight mode. This is the opposite of finding our calm in life's storms.

The second part of the Wim Hof Method involves the cold. I feel so honored to guide people into finding joy, truth, relief and transcendence in this ice bath. There's intimacy in the work we practice prior to cold immersion. We do this by tapping into the mammalian brain and using the eye gaze to send calm, kindness, and love without words. This is accomplished by looking into another human being's eyes and sharing three breaths, or hugging and sharing three breaths. This induces the desired state of intimacy, trust and, safety. This trust and safety become very valuable during times of panic, and we know that we can send calm and kindness through this often forgotten channel. This works with any mammal and is a major reason equine therapy works.

In completing the Advanced Wim Hof Certification, we were working in the ice bath to practice these techniques. The exercise looked like this:

1. Two minutes in a 37° F (2.7°C) ice bath.
2. Getting out for two minutes.
3. Completing more two minute-immersions.
4. Two minutes out.
5. Two minutes in cold repeated twice, each followed by two minutes out.

During the first round of this practice, as I had done hundreds of times before, I only noticed the water to be slightly colder that I normally practice. It was hundreds of pounds of ice and just a splash of water.

It was during the second round of this protocol where I found and practiced my panic. I completely submerged my head under the water for 15 seconds and when my head came up I entered into hyperventilation panic. I took in very quick, uncontrolled gasps of air, which was very unusual for me.

I wasn't prepared for that; I didn't know was happening. While my head was under, everything seemed normal. I was blessed with seeing my panic in a controlled, safe environment. During my panic, I looked up and caught the gaze of my instructor, Kasper (@kasperfocus on Instagram). In his eyes I found kindness. He sent calmness through this nonverbal communication channel. He peered into my soul. He said without words, "You're okay," and smiled. I smiled in return, and my panic stopped. In fact, I forgot to shiver and suffer. This all happened in less than five seconds. Powerful!

After all the breath work, in our survival response to the ice, we revert to the reptilian brain (which we will discuss in Chapter 16). For instance, when I was panic-stricken, I had the opportunity to turn off the human brain. We will discuss in detail later, but know that this is a safe space where anxiety and worry and addiction to all the negativity cannot exist. There is no future or past, just the ice centering our minds and bodies. We are forced to be in the now and we are truly present. It is here that we enjoy true mindfulness. It is in this space where we can just be. Our instructors call it high stakes meditation. We find joy in the ice, and in the ice you find your way through another door to truth and bliss. Pain is the penance that earns passage to this new part of your life's map.

The ice hacks the body's ability to make serotonin. This means there is literally joy in that ice to be found. Also, we find here a pause in life's hurricane. We find a place of repose in the frigid waters.

Having guided many people through this process, it's crazy to see the first 30 seconds of panic. By reminding the ice bather to smile, relax, and surrender, they begin to find calm. When we have our bather breathe out for a long 10 seconds, then calm in the body can be produced at will. Relaxation follows as we watch their panic melt away into a smile. A new power within is uncovered. A sense of accomplishment comes in surviving something very scary. On the other side of worry, anxiety and Fear, live truth, bliss, self-confidence, and exhilaration that can only be found walking through these scary doors.

After two minutes, the body is relieved and smiles continue. The body feels amazing. Lives are changed by breathing and icing together as a tribe.

As Wim Hof himself taught me in my time with him, the breath can save our lives if needed. This is why practicing and becoming a master of the breath is paramount in commanding Fear to work on our behalf.

FIFTEEN

The Breath that Saved My Life

This is the story of how one breath actually saved my life. I don't mean this as a euphemism. One breath literally saved my life.

Walking down the tarmac to the airplane, I was going to skydive with seven of my other friends. We did this many times at Skydive San Diego. The day before, we graduated from military free-fall school. This was the day we got to jump for fun in high speed sport parachute rigs, rather than the bulky military rigs of training. Leave it to the military to take the fun out of everything.

We jumped into the airplane and sat backwards. I smelled jet fuel while sitting on the bench in the cabin. The whine of the engines increased, and I was pushed forwards onto my knees. I was sitting backwards with the seat belt through my skydiving rig.

The plane lifted off the ground as I reminded myself to smile. For it was not anxiety or Fear I was experiencing, but rather excitement. I trained my body to know that smiling meant this was good for us.

After a dozen minutes, we leveled off at 13,500 feet. I looked out the window and gave thanks to God for such a beautiful day, a month's worth of high-intensity training completed at military free-fall School; and a body and mind trained enough to jump out of airplanes solo. That helped with the Fear (we can only experience gratitude or Fear at any one moment). I chose gratitude.

The door opened to the side of the airplane. In rushed the cold air from the atmosphere into the temperate cabin. My excitement peaked.

The red light turned on. We were just a minute away from the drop zone.

The green light turned on, indicating that we could stand up and make our way to the door.

Using the three-count exit we had practiced on the ground, we leaned into the door on "One", away from the door on "Two", and on "Three", the seven of us leapt from the aircraft. We slid down, bleeding off the forward velocity from the airplane, and transitioned into belly flying to the earth.

We linked hands, flew over each other, and carried out the jump plan. We were playing Peter Pan in the sky! It was the greatest feeling of exhilaration I have ever experienced, physically!

We played until the altimeter reached 6,000 feet Above Ground Level (AGL). Then we tracked into our assigned cardinal directions to find some free air space to make a safe parachute opening. While tracking, my hands came from above my head and shifted into the tracking pose with my hands below my waist, leaning forward. I felt like Superman as I accelerated at 40 mph in search of clean air.

At 5,000 feet, I waved my hands three times to check air space above me. Then I reached for my ripcord.

I missed the ripcord.

I tried again. Still no ripcord contact.

. . .

I reached a third time. This time I looked, and noticed there was no ripcord. I had roughly 20 seconds to solve this problem while screaming to the earth at an alarming 120 mph.

I sank to my default level of training by taking a breath during stressful situations. We usually fail to rise to the best performance when stress is the highest.

I took a breath, fully in and out.

"I am in a sport rig, the drogue chute is in the bottom, you dummy, " I scolded myself.

I threw the drogue chute and I was never so relieved to have a clean canopy above my head! My parachute opened at 2700 feet, whereas 10 seconds later I would've had a major problem on my hands.

The CYPRES 2, or automatic parachute deployment system, explosively fires at 1700 feet. It is a failsafe in the event that a jumper becomes unconscious to ensure as safe a landing as possible.

Had 10 seconds elapsed, I could have easily had two canopies above me--very dangerous. This is a safety violation that bans a jumper for life, not to mention the near-death experience I avoided due to training my breath.

I don't remember when my feet touched the ground, but I remember my hang gliding instructor, Steve Wentz (Owner of Blue Skies), wisely observing, "I'd rather be on the ground wishing I was in the sky, than in the sky wishing I was on the ground."

Breath did, can, and will save lives.

In combat operations, in skydiving, in crucial conversations--no matter the situation, there's always space for a single breath. In that single breath, we revert back from our reptile brain and we approach being human again with full cognitive capacity. This means that if we can harness the breath, we can see more and think better. The trained individual can come off the line and change their point of view for clarity. The stressed and untrained person gets tunnel vision and has fewer options from which to choose. Though it may be the same situation, with the same options, lack of training blocks the mind. Remember to either find the calmest person in a stressful situation or better yet, become the master of Fear to be that calm in the storm.

SIXTEEN

Reptile Dysfunction

I invite you to learn about the most amazing computer we know of, the brain. It is time to learn more out about the Fear and stress response and what happens in the brain.

The greatest gift we can give ourselves is dominion of the mind. So, having a model of what is happening in this amazing machine can provide insight.

Four Levels of the Brain Model

1. Reptile Brain

The oldest and most basic part of the brain is the brainstem and basal ganglia. This portion of the brain is responsible for the most basic needs: food, fight, flight, making babies, and also regulating breath, temperature, and heartrate. It is also referred to as the reptilian brain.

Before the Wim Hof method, we did not know this portion of the brain and the connected nervous system could be cleansed and accessed. This claim has been documented in verified controlled studies across various universities and hospitals.

Here in our most primitive brains, we are not making sense of what we observe, but just reacting based on conditioned, subconscious programming. It is not the best brain to use to determine the optimal course of action to take in an emergency. We will discuss more on emergency planning later. Sometimes, however, tapping into the reptilian brain is a great thing.

2. *Limbic Brain (Emotional Interpretation)*

The next brain system, the limbic brain, is where emotion resides. If the body is adequately stressed (an example is a very cold ice bath), we skip the limbic brain and go directly to the brainstem. Worry, anxiety, and addiction cannot find footing here, because the body is strictly in survival mode.

The next level up is our mammalian brain, where we process the raw signal from the senses. This input is combined with subconscious programming and beliefs to begin making sense of the world and and surrounding environment. This is where we interpret emotions like Fear, anxiety, worry, and happiness. From making sense of these emotions, the amygdala and other glands will produce stress hormones to tell the body we aren't safe. The hormones then shut down parts of the body not needed for immediate survival to include the immune system and digestion. As a result, living with Fear turned up too much limits our health.

3. *Neocortex (Human Brain)*

Finally, the most evolved portion of the brain is where language, planning, abstraction, and our perception are formed. This portion of the brain works the best when in a safe, happy, and healthy state. The more stress and Fear added, the less access we have to this higher center for thought. This is why we will be talking about the "Fear Flip" and complete our mission planning when we are calm. The best thinking occurs when we feel safe.

Will you do this with me?

Breath in deeply from the diaphragm (the belly, not the shoulders). I have included a video for you to see on the website www.yoursecretsuperpowerbook.com.

Feel the way the breath fills your lungs, the pause when you breathe in fully, and the sensation of letting the breath out in a controlled way. Notice the space between the end of the breath and the start of the next one. There can be joy in the gap between.

Please breathe with me. Let's do 10 breaths, counting backwards from 10. Again, you can see the video on your free resource page, www.yoursecretsuperpowerbook.com.

10 breaths, all the way in and all the way out.
9 breaths, all the way in and all the way out.
8 breaths, all the way in and all the way out.
7 breaths, all the way in and all the way out.
6 breaths, all the way in and all the way out.
5 breaths, all the way in and all the way out.
4 breaths, all the way in and all the way out.
3 breaths, all the way in and all the way out.
2 breaths, all the way in and all the way out.
1 breath all the way in and all the way out.

Now pause.

How different does your body feel after this exercise with breathing?

This is the first tool needed for developing mastery of our friend, Fear. We always have access to deeper breathing for deep strength and power.

For me, the change is this: I feel my inner power, focus, and wellness. It's amazing that this indescribable feeling always exists in us. All too often it is buried, literally under our nose the whole time. I challenge you to do the work and get your own inner bliss. This is what Wim Hof describes as "the inner fire".

There's a reason the Taoists consider the air as a nutrient. Feel the way the body feels rejuvenated and strong.

In various shooting courses in which my team and I participated, instructors warned us about the "caustic cocktail". They were referring to the accompanying effects of adrenaline and cortisol. Under the influence of this cocktail, your mind regresses to the reptilian mode (primitive fight or flight instinct). Remember that you don't rise to your best performance if conditions are perfect. Instead it is during extreme stressors that you will revert back to the default level of training engrained in the subconscious thought.

> **This is a critical to remember and keep in the back of the mind, because Fear closes down what we see and limits brain performance. Unless of course, we learn to hack this automatic response. You can and you will!**

When experiencing stress, remember stress is just an input, like a thought. Breathe. Remember you are the commander and get to choose what your body does next. We can make the stress "thought" smaller, more workable, and useful.

A critical move and habit is setting the deep breath anchor. The breath for me has become the start to the calm in the storm. It helps interrupt the inner monologue that says things like:

You should be further along.
Why did you screw this up?
You should be doing more.
How am I going to get all this done?
Why do you always let things like this happen?

Sound familiar?

When the inner monologue starts with these questions, breath is my chosen response to clear the negativity quickly. It's become a reminder that there is a space between the stimulus and reaction.

SEVENTEEN

Ask Better Questions

As we discussed in the previous chapter, breathing is one thing we can do in the moment to develop mastery of our friend, Fear. The second thing we can do in the moment is to turn introspective to get to the root of Fear. Here are some examples common questions that grow our Fear:

1. Why does this always happen to me?
2. Why do I always fail?
3. How can I possibly get all of this done?
4. How will I be able to find a solution to all these problems?
5. Why do I always wait until the last minute?
6. How come I'm not better prepared, smarter, thinner, (insert your thought virus here)?

These are terrible questions because when posed, it's like typing the query into the Google search bar and receiving infinite explanations to imperfections. Your brain will find answers to these self-doubting questions, making the situation worse than it actually is.

"Questions are the instrument for influence." ~Advanced Selling Podcast

The same thing applies in self-talk. What if you're in the habit of taking a deep breath as soon as your senses go on high alert? Learn this as the first, anchoring question. Secondly, ask a kind or manageable question to yourself, focusing on what you want instead of what you hope to avoid.

Much better examples of the kinds of questions to pose are:

1. What's one little thing I can do right now to improve my situation?
2. How can this situation serve me?
3. What's the lesson to be learned here?
4. What's the opportunity this challenge is affording me right now?
5. What's the best thing that's happened to me today?
6. What's something I completed recently about which I'm really proud?

These questions refocus the mind to the land of abundance, kindness, and love, instead of scarcity, shame, self-cruelty, and ultimately Fear. Focus the mind and move towards to what you truly want.

Have you heard people talk about what to do if your car is out of control? Steer into the skid, but also force your eyes to look where you'd like to go. Otherwise, you inevitably stare at the thing you want desperately to avoid, and because of this target fixation, you fulfill the worst-case scenario. You have the ability to concentrate on what you want because the focal point grows. Therefore, be careful where you place your precious attention and energy.

"The antidote to Fear is action." ~Napoleon Hill

The antidote to worry is also action. As a long-time CrossFit athlete, before every workout we hear the "3, 2, 1...go!" If you CrossFit, you probably are feeling a bit of anxiety even picturing yourself in that start position. Anticipate the start of the workout, knowing that it can be painful. You know the rigor will test your limits as you compete against classmates or competitors. But, as soon as you start to move in the workout, the worry goes away. Your body takes over. It knows what to do. It's done it hundreds or thousands of times. And now, you know what to do without much thought, because the muscle routine is familiar.

Here's a sample of my inner monologue:

> *-Brian, come on! Get your stuff together already!*
> *-Come on! How come you haven't done this already?*
> *-You should be further along!*

What is that voice? To experience hot and cold, you don't need an inner monologue.

It. Just. Is.

There's an excerpt from Michael A. Singer's book, *The Untethered Soul,* that inquires, "Who is that voice speaking?" Reading this book was the first time I realized that I'm not my thoughts. Thoughts are merely clouds. These thoughts may be true or untrue. You get to choose which thoughts you let pass and which you hold onto. It's in the imagination where we learned that Fear spreads. It's also the area in which to build mastery of it, if you make that decision.

So, the next time your inner monologue is going crazy, breathe. Then ask a better question. If it's really out of control, here is are some great questions to ask:

1. Who is speaking right now?
2. What's my next thought?
3. An even better question is, "What's one little thing I can do right now to improve my situation?"

It will be silent, and now you have a space of calm.

EIGHTEEN

Get Rescued!

Meet Jimmy Chin, actual avalanche survivor. Jimmy Chin inspires me. The video referenced below shows footage of his amazing story. He also excels at photography and mountain climbing. I discovered his work and his adventures while researching an article I wrote on surviving life's metaphorical avalanches. I introduce him to you to relate the parallel of his surviving a material natural disaster to surviving emotional and psychological avalanches. Destructive devastation or constructive metamorphosis can occur in both.

In 2015, Jimmy and his team successfully returned from climbing the Meru, arguably the hardest feat of mountaineering. The difficulty level tops the charts for several reasons. It's a multi-day climb on a big mountain and involves both rock climbing and ice climbing. His movie, *Meru*, is truly one of the most inspirational films I have ever seen about the human will, daring to push the limits, and exploring a little further. It won the 2015 U.S. Audience Documentary Award at the 2015 Sundance Film Festival.

The video shared on www.yoursecretsuperpowerbook.com is the reason we are talking about Jimmy and his work. All of this almost didn't happen. Watch the video about learn.

Jimmy survived being engulfed by an avalanche. This was huge. Thousands of tons of ice and snow exploded and poured out of the bottom of this avalanche.

He survived an actual avalanche and miraculously walked away. Most people are never seen again, buried alive, and left crushed, cold, and in complete darkness. This is why I use the analogy of buried alive in an avalanche to describe these soul-crushing and life-changing events.

The adventurers who play in this arena spend a lot of time practicing what happens when an avalanche event happens. They practice using transponders, search techniques, and quick reaction drills in the event that worst case scenarios occur.

Do you know how someone who gets buried alive by an avalanche gets out?

A well-practiced team is how that works. The person engulfed by thousands of tons of snow cannot move. The ability to draw breath quickly weakens. Often, orientation suffers severely. There is no way, after surviving amazing G forces, to self-rescue. Good luck digging out of that. The most important piece of survival gear is the transponder. Its job is to alert the team with the location to start digging. A viable team is absolutely vital to successful rescue attempts.

If people in actual avalanches need a rescue team to get back to safety, why even consider digging out of life's avalanches alone? To the subconscious mind, the body doesn't know the difference between physical avalanches and the emotional ones. Please know that self-rescue from the most epic life avalanches is unrealistic, unsafe, and unkind, especially to one's self.

. . .

We need each other.

Physical injuries and physical avalanches are similar because others can see the event and effects of these life explosions. Carrying trauma from emotional avalanches is visible when uncovering scars. Even then, if there is no capacity for compassion and empathy, understanding the lasting trauma can be elusive.

As survivors we uniquely can see other. A spooky, awesome way of finding each other happens. This is the reason why Sherpa is in the title of this movement. We are a tribe that survives together, much like the Sherpa tribe that lives on the ceiling of the planet. It's my hope and prayer that we can thrive, together, even while passing through danger.

It's like the quote from *Harry Potter and the Order of the Phoenix*:

Luna Lovegood: *"They're called Thestrals. They're quite gentle, really... But people avoid them because they're a bit..."*
Harry Potter: *"Different. But why can't the others see them?"*
Luna Lovegood: *"They can only be seen by people who've seen death."*

You have seen a different kind of death. The death of a dream, a relationship, a lesser version of ourselves, and sometimes the actual death of a loved one.

As you continue to learn about Fear and the relationship that Fear has with shame and guilt, make it easy to be rescued. Be courageous enough to say, "I'm hurting and really need some help."

Oftentimes, you are way too close to your scar to have any objective perspective. Your scar, as you will remember, is the place where you suffered a major setback, failure or loss. It takes a coach, a loved one, or someone else who has seen the *"thestrals"* in order to climb back to the light.

It's hard for loved ones, unless they are avalanche survivors themselves, to give you the kind of unconditional love and insight to come back to the land of the living and light. It takes the understanding of a fellow survivor to see and show up for each other.

I was blessed with a super-fantastic coach. She loved me when I didn't love me. She helped me realize that not all of this was my fault, and would kindly remind me of the truth when I would revert to owning all the responsibility in my avalanche. Mistakes happened and helped me realize that what I was writing and creating in my red journal - the eventual plan for Fear Sherpa - was valuable. She helped me build my confidence, because after my fall, I didn't believe in me.

So, find a coach or a professional who can be with you through this.

NINETEEN

Story A and Story B

On a fateful flight back from an amazing ski trip, I met someone who would dramatically change my life.

I sat next to this interesting guy, equal parts hippie and rocker, sporting a blonde ponytail. I noticed he was sketching mind maps, which I know to be a high level tool. This is a very effective way to organize information and gain insights.

The juxtaposition of free-flowing to highly organized data tracking intrigued me. I was compelled to ask, "Hey, man. What are you doing with your mind mapping?"

He explained that he had a client call and this was how he was organizing ideas and debriefing the meeting.

"What kind of client work do you do?" I asked, my curiosity still piqued.

He said, "I help people become architects of their language."

"What the hell does that mean?"

He looked at me and said, "Do you know what the word ABRA-CADABRA means?"

"Sure, it means magic," I said.

He explained that this word is Aramaic, the language spoken by

Christ. So the word ABRACADABRA is universally recognized in any language. It means "with these words I make real".

"Let me ask you something else," he continued, "What's a phrase that you really want to make come true?"

With confidence, I responded, "I want time, location, and money freedom... or something better."

He asked me to add soft talk words like: maybe, someday, possibly, like, or might to this powerful mantra.

I told him I wouldn't.

"Why not?" he challenged.

"I don't want this phrase to lose its power. I want to make this real."

"Exactly," he said. "I teach people the power of words and how to use architect language and solid talk."

He proceeded to introduce me to the power of spells, or groups of words of great influence. He handed me his Procabulary post card, named after his business, and gave me access to the Core Language Upgrade. After taking the course, I changed the way I communicate with others. The conversations with myself especially evolved.

I would eventually hire Mark England as a coach. During one of our sessions, we began discussing language technology called, "Story A and Story B."

Here is Story A for me, the cleaned and now accurate statement:

I got fired from what I thought was my dream job to find my actual dream job, whereby I am a guide to help people back to the land of the light, dreams, and true living. This became a powerful spell for me and my business and the Fear Sherpa Movement.

Story B, contrarily includes careless and inaccurate language:

I failed, I wasted millions of taxpayer dollars. I wasted a spot someone out of college should have had. I failed.

Which one of these stories is more appealing to you? I choose Story A all-day, every day. It's not always easy as one line of writing. It took a long time for me to really believe Story A because of the shame loop that kept running in my head. The terrible way that I talked to myself while going through the avalanche of leaving the Navy early was hard to overcome. I had listened to the small part of me that believed I was a failure and I was the mistake.

Once I grasped the deceit of such thought, I was able to listen to my higher and more enlightened spiritual self. Inevitably, I had to walk the difficult path to compassionately and courageously guide others to employ Fear, reduce or eliminate worry, and create tools to work through shame.

You get to choose your reaction in the space between the stimulus and reaction. Your choice acknowledges freedom in deciding how to react to tragic and unfair things that happen, i.e. loss, disease, and massive setbacks.

Mark and I continue working together and have become good friends. I'm so grateful for his mentorship and friendship. I welcome many more adventures and insights with this teacher.

TWENTY

Fear as a North Star

Maybe the thing you are most afraid of, or the task that keeps being put off until tomorrow, is the thing that matters the most. Time to buckle up, Buttercup. This is Fear as a North Star.

What if you had something that could be a good indicator of what the most important next thing is? Wouldn't that be great?!?

The good news is that you do. Take advantage of the journal space in your copy of *Your Secret Superpower Daily Journal* and list out your top five priorities to get done from your to-do List.

Stop reading and really do the exercise.

Right. Now!

. . .

Have any of these items ever been on your to-do list?

Hmm, isn't that interesting. Which one(s)?

Circle the one that's been on this list more than once. Why do you think that is? Is it important? Are you scared of it? If "yes," good!

Why are you scared of it? It's because it matters and there are consequences if you get it wrong. If you do it right, it could have wonderful benefits. So, this Fear you are feeling is actually a good indicator of high-leveraged and important tasks, high–level scary and high payoff. This is Fear as a North Star.

The scary items that appear to only be procrastination or indecision are actually rooted in Fear. You have just found another example of how Fear operates below our level of consciousness. Be the master of Fear, harness it, and thrive from it.

As an example, imagine feeling anxiety at introducing yourself to the attractive person at the bar. There are consequences to taking this action, right? There should be a little bit of Fear. This could be your future spouse. Think about a time when you met this same or similarly frightening Fear head-on and won. What did it feel like afterwards?

> **"Nothing in life is so exhilarating as to be shot at without result." ~Winston Churchill**

The exhilaration you earned in this case is amazing. True joy and bliss live on the other side of Fear. It is with your new friend Fear that you are able to see these opportunities. This Fear provides extra energy to survive what feels like dangerous moments and transform them into furthering your mission. Fear now has become a superpower for you. Fear is an enemy and robber for others, whereas Fear is a source of power for you...if you are courageous enough. I challenge you to find areas to practice your Fear response in a relatively safe, but scary environment. The quality of life depends on your relationship with Fear.

Let me remind you, there's a lion in you right now. Let it out and act accordingly.

Consider what American Businessman, Peter Drucker wrote in the *Harvard Business Review* article, "Managing for Business Effectiveness,"

> **"There is surely nothing quite so useless as doing with great efficiency what should not be done at all."**

If only we can change your relationship with this to-do list. One easy step is to use your friend Fear to identify the scariest tasks on your list. Practice your courage response and tackle the biggest Fear first. Save the comfortable, easy items for later when you have less energy and the consequences of not getting to them are less important. Only you will truly know this. If there are ten times when something could be done, one of these will be better than the other nine. Work on those tomorrow, but ensure you are choosing for yourself rather than Fear making this decision. Only do this tomorrow if it provides the greatest chance for success. If that's the case, you are choosing how to respond and not being controlled by Fear. To be the master of your Fear, it takes practice. Facing to-do list tasks practices courage. Change this important story.

TWENTY-ONE

Worry is Not a Performance-Enhancing Drug

As you have read, being the best possible EOD Officer was my North Star for a long time. It almost didn't happen. I almost failed the very first division of schooling. I let my worry affect my performance during the first major practical exam, Ordnance Identification.

With an engineering and science background, I aced the first few written tests of school. The first practice test involved studying and identifying projectiles, rockets, grenades and other munitions. Then I had to explain the hazards of each one and what precautions to observe. Of vital importance, such safety steps had immediate application during training. These very hazards could inflict permanent damage outside of combat conditions. Get the identification or the precautions wrong and suffer the consequences.

We started learning a whole new world of these devices and began noticing subtle differences critical to positive identification. I tend to over think things, then worry. This was all before learning how to quiet the mind and inner monologue. My worry helped make this test very challenging. I kept failing the practice tests even though I was asking for extra help. This skill was not coming to me easily.

I failed the very first real test in EOD School. This mission of years in the making, being selected, surviving the pain of dive school, might have come down to this next test. The retest was the next morning. Needless to say, I didn't sleep well that night because of the dread and the "what ifs" that tomorrow could bring. I didn't know how to stay calm in these lasting stressors.

I remember waiting for my test to be graded. I needed an 88 to pass the test and I scored something in the 70s. My heart dropped. Was my dream over?

Thankfully, my grades up to this test added up to 87.5, The statistical model used to evaluate the chances of success in EOD school needed to be 88% or higher. Due to my score being rounded to the nearest whole number, I was granted permission to continue. I could remain on my quest to become a bomb technician.

My dad shared with me what a gift I was given. He helped me realize that no amount of worry could help me perform better. In fact, worry can only reduce performance. Due to the class schedule, I needed to wait six weeks to get into the next Navy EOD Class. The men in my group would become a family. It unfolded as it was supposed to. Armed with this new perspective, I retook the Ordnance ID, and passed. The stress and challenge of the rest of EOD training still weighed on me, but I was different. I possessed an outlook that would prove very valuable to the rest of my life.

Get away from worry and focus on the pressure of a deadline, the pressure of delivering a great performance. Work with that and harness that. Worrying and fretting are dangerous. The unbridled festering of these thoughts is a virus causing inaction under inner pressure. This is self-inflicted inner pressure.

"Take care of big things when they are little." ~Sun Tzu

In other words, keep the Fear small.

This will be addressed in great detail during the Fear mitigation section of our tools and you will learn to keep Fear small and usable. Setting limits to our friend Fear is necessary.

The first thing is breath. Inner calm in the moment is predicated on the breath.

Breathe.

It can be very helpful. It may even save your life one day. It did mine as you read in Chapter 15, The Breath that Saved My Life.

We can get away from worry and remove the focus on the pressure of a deadline or delivering a great performance. Work with that, change it from a negative to a positive. Worrying, fretting, and letting this grow can be dangerous and cause us to freeze under the internal conflict of this self-inflicted inner pressure.

TWENTY-TWO

Inner Monologue - Devil on Your Shoulder

Let's revisit the inner monologue, your self-talk. You have the ability with your words and what you focus on to increase calm, or create inner chaos based on made up stories that aren't even true. When you are stressed and fearful, even your rescuers look like the enemy. To your ego, they are. Your goal is expansion and so this part of the Fear Mastery is the most frequent arena, in which to joust with your friend, Fear.

Outward skills such as skydiving, and freediving apply to the inner Fear as well and prepare us well for the inner adventure. The inner adventure can be addressing your inner demons, insecurities, shame, guilt and other traumas. Maybe less glamorous than the outer adventure, but this inner work is where we find joy, peace and self-love. Having this knowledge will help with the motivation to learn this powerful skill set.

All these ideas apply directly to your inner monologue. This is the devil on your shoulder. You know, that voice that speaks unkindly in your head? Your inner devil shows up and tries to make you love yourself less or add more stress. You possess the ability to insert a pause, break the cycle and enjoy a wedge or a pause resulting in making a different decision with more clarity.

What is the devil on your shoulder? My confession is that I still wrestle with my inner voice. Truth be told, moving forward in this life changing work, I didn't always win the head game. In fact, some days, I still lose. But because I decide to press on, I've learned how I can apply this. I am constantly refining the map and emergency procedure for how I engage with my employee, Fear.

With D.O.P.E., or Data on Previous Engagements, snipers write down all their shots. Misses and hits form the model of the world for shooting for a particular weapon, ammo, conditions, wind, and other minutia. They write out distances, winds, and other details in the moment to easily dial in their scopes for a successful shot. An approach to dealing with Fear can be the same. If you miss, good. Expansive learning occurs if you let it.

What did I learn in this setback?

Where was the breakdown? Was I Hungry, Angry, Lonely, or Tired (H.A.L.T.)?

How will I apply this in the future?

If you build the habit and really learn from your missed shots, this is how mastery is earned. You don't learn as much from your wins, but I can tell you all the times I blew myself up in EOD school (in practice of course). Never, will I ever make that same mistake again. It was painful to fail in front of peers. These setbacks are teachers. The pain can be a teacher if we learn to look for it.

Pain is not the only teacher, as other lessons can come easily. We can use self-kindness and love to move forward. I'd like us as a tribe to move away from the "no pain, no gain" ethos I used to live by. In Tim Ferriss' work, he mentions this gem of a question. "What would this look like if it were easy?"

"The unexamined life is not worth living." ~Socrates

Here are some things I would hear in my mind:

- This is never going to work!
- What if I screw this up?
- There is no way that I am the person to lead this.
- Remember the time when I failed?
- What if this question is stupid and I embarrass myself?
- How could I have forgotten to do this or messed this up so badly?
- I'll never get the (fill in the blank that I want).
- I probably don't deserve it.

Ask who is speaking here. Is it me or is it my ego trying to keep me small, safe and comfortable? Can you identify with any of these phrases?

Time for an emergency procedure.

1. Name the voice talking as something else or the personification of Fear itself. Identify the actual feeling (worry, doubt, procrastination, terror, anxiety or nervousness). Remember, this isn't even me talking, just a thought most likely isn't even true. Create distance as the non-attached observer.
2. Gratitude. If you have read this far, congratulations! When these phrases are whispered, they are your

teacher. These are opportunities to excel, and expand your mastery.

3. What is the positive tense of the limiting belief. Typically, I see the simple, yet powerful negation, i.e., I don't want to fail, to feel like this, or let this happen. Changing these into positive tense questions changes the meaning and effect it has on our headspace.
4. I succeed and get to feel like this **is** happening.
5. I **do** want to succeed.
6. I **do** want to feel like this.
7. I **do** want this happen.

Here are some other questions that effectively change the inner space:

1. What if I am successful?
2. What's one little thing I can do to improve this situation
3. What's the best thing that can happen?
4. What if I **am** smart enough?
5. **If I loved myself, what would I do?**

I witnessed the inner voice, the devil on my shoulder, affecting my performance. At the shooting range, after a missed shot, I'd get really angry at myself. I'd curse a bunch and then let that last shot affect my next one. I would continue to berate myself as an idiot for missing the mark in the first place.

This was a crazy method using hate and Fear to motivate myself to shoot better. It had the opposite effect. Actually, I was making my shooting success harder because of storm of negativity I created in my mind and body. I knew I needed to silence this negative way of thinking. What you are about to read, contains the tools that I have used in silencing that small but mighty devil on my shoulder. It is my intention to grow together in silencing the self-hate together. I find this to be a daily battle, but with some easy to learn tactics, I believe we can win together we can win.

I believe that we are created in the image and likeness of God. Do you think God ever worries? Of course not! As an all-powerful, 4th-dimensional being, He already knows how our story plays out. We, on the other hand are not so lucky. There is no way that we can predict the successes, the setbacks, failures and everything in between.

Life is punctuated by events, changing conditions, and motivations that affect the trajectory of our lives. If our loving Father desires joy and peaceful life for us, why do Fear, depression, despair, hopelessness, and shame even exist? I have come to know, it's the way we forge courage. Also, on the other side of life's scary and uncomfortable doors, exists a bliss, exhilaration and confidence that cannot be given, but must be earned.

Why do we listen to that ugly voice that speaks terrible negativity? Take a minute.

No, really, stop reading! Close the book or turn off your device.

Close your eyes and think of some lies the devil has told you.

I'm serious! Close the book and do this!

These shadows describe destructive self-talk. Doesn't sound too loving, does it? Would you ask such dismal questions of someone you love and spread an infection opposite of peace and joy? It's as if these questions lead to more self-doubt, confusion and inaction. This voice seems to appear at the most inopportune times, when the stress is mounting and further obscures the truth. Then, comes confusing advice. Instead, what if we develop a winning mindset to guard against the naysayer? If you possessed the ability to quiet this voice and devote your focused mind on the problem at hand, how much more effective and inspirational could you be? The truth is, you are called to silence the devil by taking away his power.

Let's stop the him together. Is it okay if I share with you a way that I have found to conversely encourage the angels on my side? Here are the steps I'd love to share with you.

1. Realize that you are not your thoughts. The critical piece to your inner peace is the awareness that this voice is not us, does not define us, and can actually be controlled.

The first step is to recognize the arrival of the devil on our shoulders. Energy is building inside and must be released. I find saying out loud exactly what I'm feeling to be a wonderful relief valve. In fact, call on someone you love, be vulnerable, and admit what you are experiencing. This is a great way to let your body and brain know it is okay to feel Fear, shame, pressure, etc.

If you developed a mantra, say it now! Mine is, "Get behind me Satan! [I don't have time for this today!]" Matthew 16:23, NIV.

2. The brain-body connection is an extremely important relationship. At times, the brain leads the body, and other times, the body can lead the brain.

Yogis instruct in yoga classes, that the connection between the brain and the body is the breath. My friend Danette talks about crisis meditation. I mention her here because she was the teacher who gave me my first mantra and used yoga and meditation to work through my trauma and build self-love.

Our most stressful moments may not be the best opportunity to intermittently practice meditation. On the other hand, what if as a daily practice, you begin with meditation? But, Brian isn't yoga and meditation all hippie, woo-woo crap?

Let me ask you a question. If after you turn off and restart your computer, does the computer perform much better? The brain must rest like any other muscle in the body. The brain doesn't rest during the day, doesn't rest while watching a movie, and not even during sleep. Yoga, meditation, and prayer can provide this rest period and help your mind return to an optimal state. Plus, after a year of listening to very successful entrepreneurs, top performers in music and sports, a very common theme they share is a practice of morning meditation or prayer.

Here is a good link to get you started on your path to resetting your mind everyday: (www.yoursecretsuper powerbook.com meditation) Just 10 minutes a day can have a profound effect that alters brain chemistry, reduces cortisol, the stress hormone, and increases testosterone production naturally.

During my time at military free-fall school, I learned that I'm scared of jumping out of airplanes. But I still have completed thirty-seven jumps. The Fear never went away, but what I learned was there is always time for one deep breath to calm the mind and remember the visualization of the flawless jump for perfect execution. The other trick is to look at the wing and not the person jumping out before you. I don't know, there's just something about watching someone else jump from 12,500 feet that really freaks me out.

These uncomfortable experiences teach techniques that can be applied to the classroom, sales calls, presentations, and conversations such as asking a crush for a phone number, or telling someone you love them for the first time. I highly recommend your version of sky diving, regardless of what form it takes (activities that scare the crap out of you!). I promise after overcoming your Fear, free-fall is one of the most exhilarating experiences. Once you have tasted flight, you too will understand why the birds sing.

Remember this feeling in the next stressful situation. If you train harder than you fight, the battle will be easier. Also, the more you practice being uncomfortable and quieting the devil is directly proportional to the rate at which you will quiet your mind. Then you learn to appreciate these feelings for the best possible execution for action. Who knows, could this be the feeling before the most amazing thing you have ever accomplished?

3. Mantra. I don't like a fair fight. What I mean is that you will never be in a situation and say, "Wow, I am over-prepared and over-trained for this!"

How do we stack the deck against the devil on our shoulder? The answer is to develop a winning mantra. When I was a professional sales consultant, before every sales call, I used to repeat two things that I learned from the Advanced Selling Podcast:

1. I am totally detached from the outcome of this meeting and my market is abundant. I will do everything possible to ask good questions, understand the needs that drive an outstanding presentation in the customer's terms and ask for the business.

2. But for whatever reason, this situation may be unwinnable. Nonetheless, I must remember that there are so many opportunities available. This intention allows me be to be a true consultant, someone committed to providing as much value possible, solving the problem, and make them look like a hero.

See how this is different than trying to sell? The belief changes behaviors which in turn, changes outcomes. As developed by inspirational speaker, Tony Robbins:

> **"I now command my subconscious mind to direct me in helping as many people as possible today to better their lives, by giving me the strength, the emotion, the persuasion, the humor, the brevity, whatever it takes to show these people and get these people to change their life now!"**

I added my very own powerful third mantra that has served me well. It is powerful, effective and it works. I hope it is a useful example for you:

3. I am, exactly as I am, exactly what is needed today.

When the chips are down, you will not rise to your highest level of performance, but rather to your default state. This default state is somewhere between the automatic subconscious and the easy-to-do state. Notice I didn't say, top peak performance. Although it is possible to achieve that level of inner calm when the storm rages the hardest, it requires diligent and mindful practice. Ideally, this will be the automatic, no-thought-required state during emergencies. That's the level needed to get to for the most effective employment of mantras. Practice this when the stakes are low and then when they are high...it will become your new default response, especially useful when it matters the most. How you are in small matters is how you will bc in large matters.

Encourage your angel on your other shoulder by cheering yourself on with your own unique, kind and empowering mantra!

"If you find yourself in a fair fight, you didn't plan your mission properly."
~David Hackworth

Or to put it another way:

"Stack the Deck!!!"
~Fear Sherpa

TWENTY-THREE

Prevent the Hurricane in the First Place

I find there are two types of Fear:

In-the-moment Fear, e.g.:

1. Car accidents
2. Skydiving
3. Personal introductions
4. Public speaking

And long-term Fear that present agonizing examination, such as:

1. What if I fail?
2. What if people find out I'm an impostor?
3. What if I'm not good enough?
4. What if I go broke?

The same thing is true with creating inner calm. The best way to mitigate the effects of a hurricane would be to prevent it in the first place. The storm may be raging on the outside, but inside it is calm. Get to the inner calm by not only knowing what to do in the moment, but also knowing what to do leading up to the moment.

Self-Care

If you are reading this book, chances are that you have stress in your life. You'd like to improve your relationship with Fear. It takes a lot of courage to want to change those things. I imagine that if you have gotten this far in the book, you want to do important things with your life. Check in your resources for this tool under www.yoursecretsuperpowerbook.com.

In order to do this important work, your life's work, you need to take care of yourself. Tend to the inner sanctum that is your thoughts and physical body. How do you prevent a body from being too stressed? Breathing is nice. Breathing parlayed into a meditation practice where you learn to be present is great. Experiment with this:

- Take 30 breaths, Wim Hof style
- Here's another amazing tool, music. What's your favorite song? Tim Ferriss shared that one of the ways that he learned meditation was playing his favorite song and sitting mindfully while listening to it.

Sit down and notice how the ground feels on your feet, the way your sit-bones contact the earth. Observe the way the breath goes in through the nose and out the mouth. Notice the sensation of breath at the top of the inhalation. Feel between the pause, inhale and also at the exhale, between breaths. You could do this for a song. This is such a great way to get into meditating.

***If you want more on meditation see Tim Ferriss' Blog on meditation as part of the tools I included for you under www.yoursecretsuperpowerbook.com.

. . .

Mindful Eating and Drinking

Also, in your cup of tea or coffee in the morning, how does the mug feel in your hand? What does the aroma smell like? What does the liquid feel like as it passes over your tongue? How does it taste? Describe the sensation you get when the warm liquid passes through your throat on its way to the stomach. There's an opportunity to be mindful every time we eat or drink.

ABRACADABRA! Just like that, you just learned two ways to meditate.

Meditation, The Gift of Silence

It is in silence where we touch divinity.

The thing with meditation is that it doesn't have to be this fancy thing. As we just explored together, mindfulness can take many forms. This is a gift we can give ourselves any time we need. It's powerful and it's been in us all along!

The silence is buried inside and for many, this ability to find calm and a reset is dormant. You have the power, and now the permission to explore this inner space. I heard a great quote in prayer the other day, "If you cannot handle the silence in yourself, why would you inflict that on the rest of the world?"

It's a good question.

I find that with meditation my favorite way to do this is definitely in nature. Outside with the birds chirping, feeling the warm sun is beautiful and connects you to your environment.

On Sundays in Richmond, I lead a breath and ice practice in the Wim Hof style. In the breathing cycles, there is a period where after 30 -50 breaths, we meditate with empty lungs. The space between the breaths, sometimes more than two minutes, holds peace and bliss. All this happens on the boat dock, just over the water of the James River with the birds fluttering, the fish jumping and the sun shining. What a gift. What a great way to reset and reload before the start of the week together.

In the body there is the sympathetic nervous system, responsible for the fight or flight reactions for survival. In this fearful state, the body does not allocate resources for recovery and immune function. The body does this because all available energy goes to surviving the saber tooth tiger attack. This is why you must learn to be the master of your Fear...for your health and longevity depend on the ability to be calm.

Meditation helps with recovery and getting more into the parasympathetic nervous system. I have seen and believe that there is a compound effect that happens with stress or calm. Some of my friends who are athletes wear a fitness tracker called the Whoop. This wrist device measures sleep quality, heart rate variability, pulse, workout volume and other markers to deliver a composite physical readiness score. Meditation helps with the readiness.

It's so cool leading this Wim Hof Practice with others, because for a long time I practiced this method by myself up on a roof deck. I would take my "heavenly coffee" to the roof and watch the sunrise as the eagles and ospreys glided. This is where I continue to start my day with breath, meditation and my coffee. It's absolutely beautiful and now I get to share this with my tribe.

I want to review my favorite ways to meditate:

1. Pause after three or four rounds of the Wim Hof Method.
2. Ice-bathe, going through the panic and finding the calm breath. On the other side of this is bliss, learn transcendence in this high stakes meditation.

Concentrate on the body. Close your eyes and smile.

Read this paragraph first, then try the above steps again. Breathe through the nose and keep the awareness on the wind passing through the bridge of the nose.

Pause at the top and let the air fill your head up to the third eye and bring your awareness to that part of your body.

Let the breath out slowly and gently and as the breath passes through the bridge of the nose, sink your awareness lower in your body. Go from the top of the head to then the chest, followed by the legs and finally the feet.

Breathe into the top of your head, pausing at the top and feeling your heart beating softly. On the breath out, bring the awareness back to your feet. Hold the awareness of the top of the head, the feet and the softly beating heart.

In this inward awareness, you are alone with inner silence. With each breath, become more and more relaxed. With each breath, open your heart more fully to Source, God or the Universe, and enjoy being connected to this abundance of love, bliss and wisdom.

A few times I have experienced such bliss in this space that when the 10-minute timer goes off, I want to go again and can't believe ten minutes have passed.

Consistency is critical. The more committed to a daily ten minutes, the better the calm and the bliss become. Enjoy!

The best part is this calm lives in you and you can go there anytime.

Think of this as hygiene. You wouldn't skip brushing your teeth everyday, right? Then why miss out on flossing your mind? I believe this 10-minute pause essential to mental health. Don't be a slob, floss your mind every day!

I started using a device called Muse, which is a head band with a sensor to measure brain waves during meditation. Here are some different states that I've noticed while meditating are:

1. **Monkey Mind:** The mind races and the inner monologue runs unkindly and out of control. The meditation is hard here. The Muse system plays a violent rainstorm when we are in this state. I used to hate being stuck in this state with my eyes closed and chasing calm. After many months of meditation, I know that when the mind is like this, I really need the quiet time because I

have subjected my body to too much stress. Even though the meditation feels like work, I need the mental flossing more than ever here.

2. **Calm:** The Muse makes soothing rain noises. It becomes easier to meditate because the practice starts to become enjoyable. The sounds of light drizzling of the rain are nice as well.
3. **Deep Meditation:** The brain quiets, the body relaxes and as I slide into deep relaxation, I can hear the birds start to chirp. Now the true bliss of meditation starts. The concentration for me in the breath, the heart beat and the body awareness produce a really nice experience and reset. Having practiced with Muse for over 90 days and getting real time feedback on my meditation, I can now go to this calm whenever necessary. I can find this place in winter while Wim Hoff-ing in the James River in 40-degree water, I can find it during difficult workouts and even during uncomfortable business or relationship situations. Knowing how to get to this state during the day becomes a great gift. Once again, you can be the calmest person in the room. What a gift to give yourself!

Transcendence

In the things that cause us pain and discomfort, there can be a door through which to pass. In this passing we find transcendence, of turning suffering into pain, finding the calm center in the eye of our proverbial storms. This place has bliss and truth, awareness of pain, but allows you to be significantly detached from it.

The ice taught me this. During the winter, spending time in the James River, I began experimenting with 20 minutes in the 40-degree flowing water. In some ways it was much harder than the simple ice bath. The ice bath allows cheating in the forming of a micro-layer of warmed water. With the flowing river there is no place to hide or take a shortcut. For many of these cold-water sessions, I would intentionally keep my hands out of the water, mostly because the hands hurt the most in the cold for me.

After the meditation streak, I could find the strong center of the birds chirping while cold and even there, find peace. In bringing awareness to the gut and stomach along with calm, easy breathing, the pain subsided and I even found some bliss. I knew that I had discovered my way to the other side of the door. I invite you to this side of the door of discomfort because on the other side is truth, bliss, exhilaration and pride.

> **"If we can find joy in ice....we can find joy anywhere!"**

This is a skill and an ability that applies not only in the ice, but to finding joy in the discomfort of daily challenges. This is a superpower we all possess. It's buried and lies dormant in far too many people and for too long. All it takes is for you to close your eyes, quiet the busy, turn down the noise, put the phone down and just be in it. Touch divinity in silence.

Floating

The ability to find calm in the storm is invaluable. An even more effective tool is to prevent the storm in the first place. What if you could calm the mind, silence the inner monologue and let your body relax? This tool that I have grown to love is float therapy, in which floating in a pool of skin temperature water, without light and without distraction.

In this safe space free of the hustle and stress of life, I give myself the gift of looking inwards for an hour or more at a time. After trying many things, floating has become a vital tool in harnessing Fear, working through issues and finding inspiration and forgiveness.

The four grandest treasures I returned home with from my floating sessions are:

1. A silent inner space where my inner monologue goes away for many days. The devil on my shoulder leaves for a much-needed break.

2. Forgiveness for an adversary who needlessly made my life harder to prove I didn't belong to this special community. I was able to let go of my resentment and hate and finally start healing because of an imaginary conversation I had with him in the float tank.

3. "I whispered, Fear in the hands of a master becomes a superpower, but Fear in the hands of the untrained can be deadly," during one of my float sessions.

4. The start of my TED talk was practiced in front of my future audience. I saw myself entering the stage in an amazing way. I found that inspiration while floating.

Journaling

Tim Ferriss talks about the 5-minute journal and the bouncing rock or the monkey mind. The mind is a terrible place for remembering things you have to do. The brain is wonderful for solving problems, it can be good for imagination or creating new things. But the things we are most worried about, get it out on paper. Release it.

I created a journaling practice that turned into *Your Secret Superpower Daily Journal*, a companion guide to this book where you can take your Fear mastery to the next level.

Here's the outline:

1. Quote of the day.
2. Three things for which you are grateful.
3. Three areas where altitude was gained.
4. My top five biggest tasks for the day.

5. Circling the task of which I'm most afraid. It will be the most important or produce the greatest returns.

6. Lesson learned or opportunities to grow, results and lessons from experiments.

7. The helpful mantra or kind question.

I struggled for a long time with insomnia. What I learned was that my brain was racing with all the things that I worried about getting done the next day. If I would take out my calendar, schedule my day and also write about the critical tasks, I could rest easy. If the concerns are written down somewhere, there's no need to worry because they are scheduled and addressed.

Play. Don't forget to play. Play is the single greatest stress reliever that we have. Throw a Frisbee, go for a walk in nature, ride waves, ride the wind, or even make up a new game with your friends.

Preparing the body and the mind before moments of stress can make you the calmest person in the room. You will have more options, because you are the one using more of the human brain and less a reactive reptilian brain, responding like a lizard. Stress turns us to reptiles and relieves us of our ability for evolved thought.

Remember also that if you find boredom, you're not paying attention.

TWENTY-FOUR

Shame Prison

At some point, we must press against the feeling of discomfort and lean into our Fear. After physical or emotional trauma, regression into a protected, safe space needs to occur. When misled to believe that you either made the mistake or are the mistake, you erect a shame prison around yourself. This comfortable shame cave is an illusion that feels safe, yet is extremely dangerous. This is how atrophy of life begins. It has to do with the story you tell yourself behind shameful activity or circumstance. You are both the gatekeeper and criminal of your prison. It is locked from the inside as a way to heal you from your wounds physically, emotionally and spiritually.

Picture a solitary confinement prison cell. In your mind, you have constructed the walls with the bricks of shame, bonded them together with the cement of guilt and locked yourself in with the iron door of Fear. You confine yourself and will decay to dust if you do not choose to rage against this process.

Let me illustrate this point as a fun fact. Did you know that a seven-ton circus elephant can learn to stay captive on a tiny leash with a single stake? Clearly these massive creatures far outmatch their shackles. Why do they stay captive? It begins with conditioning them when they are very small. They came to know that the stake and leash keeps them confined. As they grow bigger and stronger, they never try to pull against the stake because they have learned that it is an exercise in futility. In fact, once fully grown, with very little effort, they have the ability to pull against the tiny stake and taste freedom.

It's interesting the story these elephants have learned that keep them tethered to a flimsy stake. How does this apply to your life?

Our shame and Fear prison is the same. We constructed the walls at a time when we needed seclusion and isolation, but the door isn't locked. It could be that we tell ourselves, like the elephant does, "I'm stuck here." All that's needed, however, is to push against the unlocked prison door, from the darkness of shame into the light of freedom.

Summary of Ice

1. It's almost impossible to self-rescue from an avalanche, in mountaineering or in life. How can you employ the use of rescue equipment for your escape? Use journaling, coaching, finding a team, family or other survivors as tools for rescue. Some people haven't built the courage to be with you in this struggle. Be prepared for that as well.

2. Develop a strong posture in dealing with your setback. You have the right to feel and experience whatever you are feeling. Remember, the rules are what you enforce.

3. It's okay and even healthy to seclude yourself into a safe place, a shame prison, after a major physical or emotional injury. On the other hand, it is unhealthy to stay there forever. Remember to treat yourself with kindness as you climb out of your avalanche.

4. Remember that shame prisons are locked from the inside. You are the gatekeeper and you alone hold the keys to your freedom and your epic life. Every choice made avoiding resistance, is us choosing to regress deeper into shame. Choose wisely. It matters.

5. A major forgotten superpower is hidden right under your nose. The nose and deep belly breathing can help us to transcend pain,

stress, worry, self-doubt and create space for us to make a different decision. It's the bridge between our physiology and our minds. We have more control of our mind and body than most of us realize.

6. Expand the wedge. Practice widening the gap between the stimulus (our triggers) and our responses. It is here that true freedom resides.

UNDERWATER

TWENTY-FIVE

The Day I Ran Out of Air Fifty Feet Underwater and Was Trapped

During underwater division at EOD school, our class traveled to Jacksonville, Florida, to conduct diving operations and training on larger Navy ships. This would be one of the last times my whole EOD school class would travel together. trips with these amazing warriors.

One of the training days involved my classmate Alan and I as a buddy diving pair. Our mission was to conduct a jackstay search. This search pattern is perfect for sweeping larger areas to recover classified material, weapons, or sensitive gear dropped over the side. Imagine, two weights with a line measured in between along with lines with buoys so that the dive supervisor could keep track of our search progress. It was my duty to move the weights forward through the four feet of mud. I remember having to bury myself in this silty pudding bottom in order to move one of the weights to further our search. We would search that side and then move the clump further and continue searching with our two arm lengths wide. We got to the end and move the weights again and keep searching.

If you are picturing pleasure diving with dozens of feet of visibility, this was the opposite of that. I could barely sense where the light was coming from, but that was about it. There was no seeing any of my gauges, much less the hand in front of my face. This was diving by feel.

We were making good progress in moving the search forward. Once again, I couldn't see my gauges. Thankfully my dive watch has an audible and vibratory alarm set for twenty-five minutes of searching. The alarm went off and we started ascending the water column back to the sun, visibility, and dry clean clothes. I noticed that when I would ascend to the lighter colored filth, I was getting stuck on something. I couldn't see, but I had this feeling the jackstay line itself was caught on my dive rig.

I practiced finding calm and slowing my breathing. The calmer I remained, the more air and time I would have to solve this problem. With my dive knife out ready to cut away the line, I squeezed Alan for his attention and then to ask him to help me untangle this situation. I knew also that I must be getting close to running out of air.

As Alan is pulling the huge loops of the daisy chained jackstay line from my second stage regulator, I took my last breath of compressed air and then felt a hard stop to my breathing. Scuba breathing is very effortless and I found this new sensation, running out of air alarming. Never had I breathed down a bottle during a dive. We pushed right to the limit of our equipment that day. Also, I just want to thank the person who daisy chained the line, as those loops should have been hand sized, and not the size of my shoulder and regulator. Murphy's law, which states that anything that can go wrong will go wrong, was messing with us really badly that day.

My tank was out and I was still under 50' of sea water. With my wetsuit and shoulder injury, I couldn't turn my J valve which provides another 500 psi of air, which was plenty to get to the surface. I yelled underwater, "Alan, flip the J-valve."

He did this easily and I took the best single breath I have ever earned. We finned our way to the surface, back to the clear water, bright sun, and safety of the boat. Grateful for so many things that day.

Once again, the discomfort is the teacher. Asking for help and knowing that I was going to be okay helped the situation from becoming a diving emergency. It was challenging to remain calm with our gear challenges and patiently wait while the situation was being fixed. During dive school they taught us to harness the panicky feeling. If we gave into the panic and jettisoned everything to get to the surface, it would be a great way to get hurt diving. On the last breath, I couldn't just bolt to the surface. This climb to the surface should have taken 2 minutes to do safely. By remembering that I get to control my reaction, we prevented injury and avoided getting the bends. In you are unfamiliar, the bends or its formal term, nitrogen narcosis, is when the dissolved nitrogen bubbles come out of solution in our blood. These bubbles can cause stroke and irreversible damage to the nervous system. It is a painful and dangerous medical condition.

Once again finding calm in the storm saved my life and it will yours as well.

The Wedge

Freediving explores the majesty of the ocean with a single breath, unfettered by equipment. In the book, *Deep*, author James Nestor claims the maximum mode to explore the ocean in 300 feet of seawater, is through freediving. Furthermore, he believes the body is uniquely purposed to thrive in this environment.

> **Warning: Freediving is dangerous and should never be attempted without proper training and supervision. Do not ever try this alone.**

Therefore, unless you are properly trained, I am recommending just reading about it and saving the freediving to the professionally trained. If you are not certified, practice on land lying down or at least sitting. The breath is powerful and needs to be respected.

This is an instance of honoring the gift of what Fear is trying to do on your behalf. Many people have died exploring the ocean this way. My goal is to make your life more fulfilling and to thrive. This is hard to do if you push beyond your healthy limits and exit this life before your time. This carries over to anything dangerous. I'm not saying don't do it, but know the risks, have a plan, and move forward smartly.

Just as the summit is the half-way point in climbing, the depth we reach underwater signals the time to turn around. The hardest part is clawing back to the surface when the body is screaming to breathe. The acidity of the blood is painful and your will to live is the most powerful, when you are agonizing for that clean, deep breath of fresh air. Taking your final breath underwater does nothing to make the earth cleaner and brighter than we found it. Please be smart.

The human body has the ability to be pressurized by seawater to incredible depths, the physiology of the body is able to explore up to, and even past 300 feet. Especially at those depths, a single breath can be a better way even than using the SCUBA technique. With freediving, there are no equipment nor decompression issues to deal with because it's only a single lung full of nitrogen. SCUBA packs a ton of nitrogen and one must plan ahead at these depths to come home safely. Freediving has its own challenges. Preventing emergencies and mitigating risk is the key to survival.

This sport is a wonderful exploration of the dance between stimulus and reaction. Specifically in freediving, the urge to breathe is sometimes deceiving. I heard Dave Asprey, accomplished biohacker, creator of Bulletproof Coffee and CEO of the Bulletproof Company, mention that when the body is 90% away from dying in cold or lack of oxygen, it feels like it's going to expire. In reality, however, we are a long way from death.

With pre-breathing and packing in a bunch of oxygen, the urge to breath is caused by a buildup of carbon dioxide (CO_2). A diver starts to get air-hungry from the higher concentration of the CO_2 in the blood. The gulping, swallowing, chest and stomach convulsions indicate it is time to head back to the surface. These urges will subside. It is when the second set of urges occurs that it signals the need to breathe. Most get to the air. Again, do not go it alone. Freediving should be done with a buddy and only after taking a reputable training course.

THIS IS EXTREMELY DANGEROUS AND YOU CAN FOOLISHLY KILL YOURSELF IN THIS SPORT. Honor your Fear; freediving is extremely dangerous.

Once the body craves oxygen, the spleen will release a reserve of oxygen-rich blood to the rest of the body. I like using this example because the urge to breathe is an important indicator for our survival, but ultimately we choose how to respond to this stimulus; stay or ascend to the surface.

TWENTY-SIX

Stimulus ->Freedom->Reaction

Over the years, the work of Austrian psychiatrist and psychotherapist, Viktor Frankl, changed my life. It seeded the idea that would give birth to my new relationship with Fear and other resistances. The idea and inspiration came from my adopted Jewish Auntie Talya (T), who said,

> *T: Where are you getting this stuff from?*
>
> *Fear Sherpa: This is how I'm learning to turn suffering into just pain and metabolizing this setback.*
>
> *T: In all my years of therapy, I've never seen this before. You got something here, kid.*

I'm sharing this because it takes inspiration and faith in yourself sometimes; faith from those who already see you as your future, perfected self. We talked about Frankl's work very early on in this conversation, because this was the inspiration in mastering Fear and knowing you always have a choice in how to react, even if trudging through Hell.

That's the choice in life, as taught by Viktor Frankl's *Man's Search for Meaning*. Frankl wrote that even in the most horrific of circumstances, a prisoner in a Holocaust camp, one can find freedom. It is impossible to prevent terrible things from happening. You can, however, master your reaction. That is the freedom.

I believe and have benefited from knowing that I can choose how I respond to this Fear and even play in the space between feeling Fear and transmuting that into flow or even bliss. See www.yoursecretsuperpowerbook.com for Will Smith's Skydiving video.

Here, actor Will Smith shares the most blissful moment of his life:

> **"God placed the best things in life on the other side of Fear... at the point of maximum danger, is the point of minimum Fear."**

I'm sharing these ideas because I want you to be prepared for when Fear shows up, what to do with it, and how the process goes. How great would it be to harness or even play with this process? It would be life changing and become even an extra source of drive and power that the untrained miss out on.

Let's play.

Do you know how to delay a sneeze? You may be thinking, no way... that happens automatically, or does it?

As the urge to sneeze comes up, press your forefinger into the bone underneath your nostrils.

Look! You did it. You have some control over your body. That's why this chapter starts with talking about free diving and how sometimes your body lies to you. With this in mind, I've discovered that Fear and its symptoms can lie as well.

Fear left unchecked operates in the subconscious. Just as you learned in preventing a sneeze, you can learn to insert a pause and decide how you will respond to the gift of Fear. This analogy and system work for shame, guilt, and addictions.

As part of my process to keep my body healthy, I will use water fasting to keep the body clean. I found this to be a great way to prevent cancer and to enjoy other amazing health benefits. The first few days are hard because the body is used to eating. Hunger pangs show up and then, after day 2 or 3, the hunger goes away. The body is designed to go long periods of time without eating and fasting turns into a very calming, or even pleasant feeling and even creates some joy. The mouth feels a bit metallic, but that's because even the tongue is becoming cleaner. The body doesn't really need food for a long time. When you become hungry the second time, then it's time to eat. The body is done self-cleansing and needs food.

I bring up the sneeze prevention, freediving and fasting because we always have a choice.

Once again, there are ways to practice experiencing a stimulus and making a different decision. You can practice your courage and therefore gain more freedom from this Fear and automatic choices your body makes without your conscious input. You choose and earn the right to be the master of your friend, Fear.

Widen the Wedge

Here is a secret to widening the wedge between stimulus and response.

I learned this through my mindfulness practice and it is how I discovered, as I like to call it, high stakes meditation. My teacher shared with me that each inhale pulls in new thoughts. Each exhale releases thoughts. That's why when holding my breath, new thoughts stop or pause. When the air hunger starts, breath is the only thing you can think about.

It's very centering. Treat the ideas that pop into your mind as clouds. Watch the clouds (thoughts/feelings) pass by as a casual observer or dig into them, scheduling time in the future to address concerns. You get to choose to be the non-attached observer.

TWENTY-SEVEN

Compound Effect

The choice you make in any particular moment, in that single moment, doesn't really matter, except it does because life is made up of these micro-decisions and all we have is the one choice now. Life is composed of these micro-decisions and success or failure is governed by this compound effect that is always happening, whether you are aware of your choices or not. Either you choose to do the homework and spend time harnessing your Fear, or you don't. The lie is that no one will ever know. Except I know when I didn't show up to the workout, the scary conversation, didn't speak my truth or execute the absolute best course of action. In the present moment, a decision must be made. Choose and act wisely, because the future depends on it. I'm counting on you to do this work.

In the words of Jim Rohn:

"I will take care of me for you, if you will take care of you for me."

I had the unique opportunity to meet Jeff Olsen, author of the

Slight Edge. He shared with me that he wanted to add one critical detail to the compound effect mindset from his book, "The individual decision doesn't matter. Except it does matter, because our lives are composed by all these little moments and all you have is that little moment." So, you are either freer or more oppressed based on how you react to these stimuli. The secret is that the decision is yours alone. It has been and always will be yours to make.

Let us choose micro-decisions to be free. Let us choose to be survivors. Avoid longing for the future of gaining freedom, thereby removing obstacles of the past. Be present with your suffering and look for ways to help others with theirs.

Think about this the next time a Fear pang, or a terrible thought happens. You get to react. Your act of rebellion can be a single breath. Bask in a feeling of calm. You possess a small advantage the untrained person doesn't have.

Maybe you asked a better question. Instead of, "How am I going to get all this done?" Consider replacing it with, "What's one little thing I can do to make this situation a little better?" Maybe you need a little calm in your life's storm. "What's my next thought?" inserts a pause and grounds you in the inner monologue by creating a period of silence.

Maybe you take a series of breaths. Maybe you see how long you can go on a breath hold. Maybe you stand up with a power pose. Check out the Power Pose under www.yoursecretsuperpowerbook.com and feel your power grow. Maybe your friend Fear is trying to give you some really important advice. Maybe what you are about to do is really dangerous and you need to find the edges of it. Maybe spend time with the source of this Fear and lean into it.

Let's say that you are feeling anxious or nervous before an important meeting or crucial conversation. Here is how to apply this:

1. Smile and allow excitement to take root.

2. Ask yourself, "Could this be the feeling I get before I do something awesome?"

3. Enjoy the exhilaration of showing up to your daily "skydive."

Maybe that feeling is your body telling you it's time to get to work and get after it. Fear gives the trained some extra energy. Congratulations! If you made it this far, you've dug in and are doing the work. After all, to the victor go the spoils. Welcome.

Summary of Underwater

1. Use the Fear Flip technique to intelligently identify where the actual danger is, and take steps to mitigate and practice these responses when calm. Remember to spend time in the positive outcome desired.
2. Apply mitigation techniques and find the ones that work best for you.
3. Practice. Practice. Practice.
4. I would rather practice 5 minutes of meditation every single day than an hour once a week. What will you do on a daily basis that supports mastery of our friend Fear?
5. Command of the breath can save your life physically or emotionally. The breath can provide clear headedness when it matters the most and when running away is the most dangerous option.

CLIMBING

TWENTY-EIGHT

Climbing with Wim Hof

Our Wim Hof Masters Class woke up hours before dawn to do something we had never done before, climb Mount Hood with Wim Hof himself while wearing minimal clothing to experience cold and altitude.

We left the parking lot at 4,500' feet at a breakneck pace under a black sky. Everyone struggled to keep up with Wim.

Wim taught us the breath he used when climbing Everest, barefoot and in shorts without acclimating.

This breath is a two-part inhale through the nose and a half exhale. Repeat until desired altitude is achieved.

The nose breath is critical for efficient production of ATP and oxygen uptake. The half exhale keeps the CO_2 high, which does a few things in the body. First, it allows us to fully metabolize the dissolved oxygen. Without CO_2 we would not be able to use the oxygen we have. Second, it increases nitric oxide, which is a powerful vasodilator. This is our built-in rescue inhaler.

Even with this effective breathing methodology, within twenty minutes or so, I was at the very back of the pack. I noticed feeling humiliation to be the last person. Dr. Trish and another classmate stuck with me through my slow, but deliberate climb.

You see, months earlier I strained my left calf and the level of my discontentment increased as I continued to climb. Make things worse, I did this climb in my Vibram Five Finger Shoes. There's no heel to these "shoes" so I began to regret this decision. In addition to the physical challenges of climbing a volcanic mountain of sand and little rocks, I was wrestling with ego. I knew that in order to enjoy this climb, I had to practice letting that frustration go. Once again, I then remembered to find the pain relief I needed and a calm mind with reliance on my breath practice. All I had to do was breath and keep climbing. I found calm and begin smiling.

I surrendered to my own pace for that day and knew I was doing my absolute best. I did in fact find joy in time to watch one of the most breathtaking sunrises I can remember. I arrived to the top, with our tribe, dancing, singing, playing music and sharing the warmth of accomplishment for completing something amazing. Seven years before this I journaled about my first mini retirement and how I wanted to enjoy learning and traveling. Looking back on this day I realized my prediction was spookily accurate, and how awesome it was that the Mount Hood climb and my writing all those years ago manifested that day.

The most elite of us climbed the 4,500' in 90 minutes and I finished as the last person in 110 minutes. I calculated that our top people were climbing at an astonishing pace of 3,000 feet per hour; as the last climber hiked a respectable 2,500 per hour. (A rule of thumb in backpacking is 1,000/hour.)

This was a great example of an inner adventure making the outer adventure much more enjoyable. The human body along with specific breathing techniques is capable of so much more that we are led to believe.

TWENTY-NINE

The Crux

Possessing this bombproof mindset is the crux of all of this. So many of us, myself included, are very cruel with messaging ourselves.

In every endeavor and every challenge, there will always be a step that is the hardest and most demanding. It is a move, task, or problem that demands our best self to rise to the challenge. In climbing, there is a term for this. It is called the crux.

The crux is the hardest move(s) on a given route. I find it fitting that climbers and mountaineers have a term for this, because these men and women possess an instinct to seek out harder and harder routes to find where their physical limits lie. These adventurers push the envelope beyond where they are comfortable into purposeful pain, because it is in the land of uncomfortable where the growth occurs!

I remember in college, when I was first starting to climb, there was so much to learn! Knots, equipment, technical jargon, falling and falling and falling again, then finally flashing my first route with help from Brian, my climbing partner. We kept it easy for the people meeting the Brian Team. I had to teach my body how to balance, twist and use grace to finesse my way to the top. Falling, then learning new techniques from my climbing partner led to a desire to run harder and harder routes. We started climbing outside and then extended to climbing trips. Brian and I developed a trust that was hard to find. We were also building the desire to seek out more difficult challenges in the sport, which naturally applied to life. These truly were some of my fondest college memories!

Why was this so much fun and why am I writing about this now? Deep down inside me, there is a yearning for something to grind against, a harder route, a more challenging race or sport to satisfy this need. Once that challenge is surmounted, a feeling of true accomplishment and the highest form of happiness is achieved, but there must be a crux to work through. If it were easy, there's no value. The harder the challenge, the greater the odds, the better the story.

I find myself in the crux of running the route that is finding and working my life's purpose. For a long time, I found myself asking the Lord, "What is it that you need me to do and what do you need me to learn today?"

After reading Ryan Holiday's, *The Obstacle is the Way,* I feel challenged to make an offer to the world and Universe with what I think I can best add. I offer to help others embrace Fear, shame, and challenges as the necessary ingredients for achieving individual purpose and making an awesome story in the process. This is the hardest challenge yet because I'm embarking on a journey away from a good life in the hopes of a great life. I aspire to a life of leading others through their life's crux in harnessing all of life's uncomfortable teachers. This is the path to forging incredible lives and people.

As in climbing or any of life's toughest obstacles to overcome, there are a few things to remember:

1. It's supposed to suck, but in the words of Senior Chief in dive school, "We love the way it sucks." What Senior Chief was preparing us for was the really hard and scary times. He was getting us ready to be warriors; to know these challenges awaited us after the comfort of the familiar brick and mortar school. He had fully trained us to anticipate survival responses to most any scenario.

In cold, fatigue, hunger and all manner of mortal pain and wounds, can you find the joy? Can you switch a light on to grow stamina, endurance, etc. rather than stumble in darkness?

Such an approach changes challenges, setbacks, and falls dramatically. The difficulties are integral to the story and without them there are no growth opportunities. What if you embrace the good parts of the journey **and** treasure the parts that make you a better you? Search for opportunities in the setbacks. What if we could expect the setbacks with a definite attitude of, "I've been expecting you. Is that the best you've got?" And if we combine this idea with 'you are my teacher and I surrender to your instruction', what a amazing outlook we have developed! In this two-idea combination, we can find the strength to not only endure, but to be better as a result.

2. Sacrifice comfort in exploration of new challenges, thereby risking failure. What is the one thing that you are 100 percent committed to that could fail? That is part of truly living. That is the truest expression of the indomitable human spirit.

I love this credo attributed to early 20th century author, Jack London:

> **"I would rather be ashes than dust! I would rather that my spark should burn out in a brilliant blaze than it should be stifled by dry-rot. I would rather be a superb meteor, every atom of me in magnificent glow, than a sleepy and permanent planet. The function of man is to live, not to exist. I shall not waste my days trying to prolong them. I shall use my time."**

I feel defiant when I read this. My imagination shows the Fear Sherpa standing in the gale force winds, leading himself and others through life's climb. Calm. Focused even though the storm and mother nature fights, he has found calm on the inside.

My desire is to leave this earth having exhausted all energy, ideas, books, and relationships in full exploration. This is in refusal to surrender to Fear. By indecision and ultimately failing to decide, a terrible decision in itself. Instead of burning bright, life is ground into dust. You were meant to thrive, which takes courage and resiliency. This book is preparing you for this amazing journey.

It's my hope that you die empty, having burned full and bright.

3. I request that you remember to pray or send good energy for me, our tribe and this mission. I intend to live and teach others how to climb the mountain of life, rescue fellow avalanche survivors no longer captive to Fear, shame, worry and the rest of Fear's minions.

It is my hope that my journey will inspire you to run the route that you deem worthy of your talents, time, and being. I find myself at the crux of this journey right now, getting started; knowing that there will be falls, pains, bad weather and many other setbacks. But, if you can learn to expect and love the setbacks, you will use these problems to grind against all the way to the summit and truly reach your fullest potential.

Warning: Once you prove to the Universe, yourself, and God that you can handle challenges, expect more. When you gain grit to endure the climb, you will naturally seek more advanced complexity and therefore, more beautiful and inspiring climbs. Also, know that all the surmounted peaks are building to your magnum opus.

Climb Away!

THIRTY

Emergency Procedure - OODA Loop by Colonel John Boyd

Colonel John Boyd was the father of air-to-air combat operations, and aircraft designer for models A-10, F-15 and F-16. He did amazing things. He is known as the father of modern aviation, as he turned air to air combat into a science. He challenged the status quo of his leadership team, tirelessly worked the data to innovate air superiority and had the courage to bet on himself. He is known to have staked his career with his bosses a few times. He fought for what be believed to be the most combat effective methods for aviators. This man understood Fear and chose to harness it. You could say he risked it all with stunning payoff.

I'm bringing this up because of his genius of the OODA Loop. This is a work of art. The acronym OODA stands for:

1. **Observe**: Notice all sensory inputs. This is being present in the chaos.
2. **Orient**: Begin making sense of the chaos and finding the pattern or something recognizable or similar to past experience.
3. **Decide**: Now that you can identify the inputs and

patterns, you can identify the appropriate emergency procedure for the situation.

4. **Act**: Execute the rehearsed emergency procedure. Remember the baseline line as the rote starting point since adrenaline and cortisol highjack your higher thought.

Allowing adrenaline and cortisol to highjack their thoughts, by the way, is how most of the population makes decisions. What if you could hack this system and make this loop smaller and smaller? What I mean is, make better decision faster, under pressure. Any idiot can rationalize perfect decisions from safety. However, in the real world, life-changing actions rely on this ability. Seek and find some efficiencies here.

Know that the **Observation** will happen and cannot be shortened. This is all of your senses monitoring the current situation.

The **Orientation** phase makes sense of outside sensory inputs. In other words, you make sense of the chaotic conditions in which you are climbing or flying, in this example. Over elapsed time, experience and repetitious practice shorten this part of the OODA loop.

The most efficient way of shaving time off crucial decisions is to already decide what the course of action will be. When safely on the ground, surrounded by experts and references, a myriad of scenarios can be thought up and addressed. Notice I didn't say, "...while traveling at the speed of Mach 2, engines aflame, freaking out and losing your mind". It's impossible to make your best decisions here, thus you have emergency procedures. They've been proven to work when it matters. Take out the noise, and focus on execution. I also find experimenting with different situations and mentally rehearsing is the difference between those trained in a Fear response and the untrained.

This is not something saved for the "special." We all can do this if we decide now to practice. That is the difference, quality of practice, frequency of this practice and the review of the results and measurement of this practice.

> *****Warning: The untrained in this situation will add extra turbulence with unbridled imagination. Decide to be a professional, and use the imagination to serve you, executing flawlessly and getting you to safety, especially when it matters most.**

Please seek the book, *Checklist Manifesto,* written by Atul Gawande, for a much deeper and thorough exploration of this potent tool.

Finally, **Act** on this decision. Once the practice and habitual repetition are completed, the hardest and most intensive parts of the OODA loop are done. The act part may only be a few seconds, but it matters how you arrived at this conclusion and chose this course of action, especially when life is in the balance. If this is truly a life-or-death moment, no amount of worry will help. In truth, you will either have success or failure. Be certain that with the given information at the time, you made the best decision you could. You did your best in that moment. Please remember this. Unkind thoughts and blame for not choosing differently come too easily in the aftermath or debrief, after-action review, particularly in the event of a mishap or casualty.

It's okay to learn from mistakes. It's not okay to think you yourself are a mistake for choosing a suboptimal solution when your "plane," is on fire. Did you do your best with the given information at the time? If the answer is "yes," it is a learning opportunity. If not, how did you get here, and how can you warn others? This can be a teaching moment, and there can be value in missing the mark.

The point of knowing and practicing your OODA Loop yields faster and more accurate decisions, undoubtedly useful while flying Mach 2, is also helpful in everyday situations. You aren't normally flying this fast so again, a situation of training harder than we will fight so the more normal challenges can seem relatively easier. The aviation community needs quantification, because imaginary scenarios occur at a mile every five seconds, whereas actual space flight occurs at a much faster five miles a second or faster. Effective decision-making-abilities are absolutely necessary because in no other time in mankind's history were humans flying this fast. Subsequently, the consequences for safe flash-decisions grow proportionally. Winging it creates preventable losses of equipment and human life. Deciding what to do in the moment on the fly for the first time is costly in terms of mental energy and time. Flying these operations and wasting resources have grave consequences. This is true in aviation, spaceflight as well as your life.

There's another way to address these known dangers. This is actually how Emergency Procedures (EP) were developed. Think about it. When do you think they construct these vital courses of action?

Is it in the moment when the aircraft engines are on fire, a crash is eminent, and stress couldn't be higher? Or do they germinate and grow in a room or simulator, when everyone is calm and the best ideas are shared and developed?

You guessed it, the latter. Why is it the second situation?

When the brain and body are calm, we can operate and make decisions with the human brain. All the resources are available and discussion and insight are possible. Ample time allows your brain to think, creatively solve problems and even see what you are blinded to in the midst of pressure. When stressed, tunnel vision regresses thought to the lower reptilian brain. A calmer brain and body have more options that the untrained cannot even see.

THIRTY-ONE

Decide When You Are Calm

How does the OODA Loop serve in the employment of our friend, Fear? Not if, but when Fear strikes you, your constructed checklist and repetitive rehearsal payoff in positive action. The OODA Loop is worthless unless put to use. Value lies in conscientious application to, Fear.

When I skydive, the act of watching someone else fall to the earth before me really scares me. Fear attacks on the ride up, much like the suspenseful ascension on a rollercoaster. Jet fumes filling my nostrils, approaching with a backward view and the roar of the engine all make for a stressful setting. Then there's the dual anticipation of exhilaration and dread of what's about to happen.

Finally, the plane door opens and chilly air invades the warm sanctuary. The red light changes to green. Something is about to happen. The plane shakes and then the first jumper is away and falling to the earth. This is the maximum Fear point for me. I know that bliss is just on the other side of this so I learned to write my very own emergency procedure for this scenario:

When I feel the first burst of anxiety, I take a deep breath and watch the earth getting smaller and smaller on the skydive roller coaster. When I feel the Fear, I breathe and remember to smile. I'm telling my body okay, I'm okay, announcing to myself the imminent fun.

When the door opens, more smiling, checking other jumpers' equipment, high fives and first bumps. When I'm in the door, my EP is this:

1. Look at the wing (I struggle watching the person jump before me, so I avoid this).
2. Breathe, I find calm this way.
3. Smile, transmute Fear into excitement.
4. Imagine a perfect exit.
5. Jump. Have faith that everything will be great, and the fun is about to happen.

THIRTY-TWO

Fear Mitigation - Fear as a Gas

In my experience, I found Fear to behave much like a gas. A gas is a substance or matter in a state in which it will expand freely to fill the whole of a container, having no fixed shape (unlike a solid) and no fixed volume (unlike a liquid). Fear behaves the same way in expanding to whatever size container we allow, regardless of the quantity of the worry, doubt or other incarnation of Fear.

Wouldn't it be great if we could keep big Fear little?

> **"Plan for what it is difficult while it is easy, do what is great while it is small." ~Sun Tzu**

This next chapter is going to show you how to do exactly this with Fear. The Navy practices Fear mitigation in Operational Risk Management. Understanding dangerous situations, managing the known risks, and ensuring the maximum margin for safety and mission success is how the Navy conducts diving, demolition and other risky jobs.

Here is a chart used by the Navy:

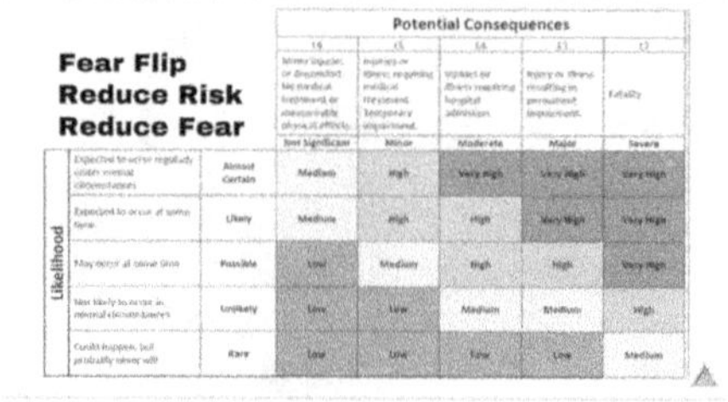

Fear Flip
Reduce Risk
Reduce Fear

Likelihood		Not Significant	Minor	Moderate	Major	Severe
		[illegible]	[illegible]	[illegible]	[illegible]	Fatality
Expected to occur regularly under normal circumstances	Almost Certain	Medium	High	Very High	Very High	Very High
Expected to occur at some time	Likely	Medium	High	High	Very High	Very High
May occur at some time	Possible	Low	Medium	High	High	Very High
Not likely to occur in normal circumstances	Unlikely	Low	Low	Medium	Medium	High
Could happen, but probably never will	Rare	Low	Low	Low	Low	Medium

You can see a larger version of the chart under www.mysecretsuperpowerbook.com. I love this chart. It made the leadership team look at the areas that were most dangerous. To complete this exercise, it takes courage to really look at where the Fear or danger actually lies. It forces a hard look at acceptable risk, in which the benefit does not justify the means. Then a better plan for risky areas can be explored in order to be safer by adding controls or mitigating actions to reduce the likelihood and severity of consequences.

A critical idea here is a time constraint. For day-to-day training requirements, no more than an hour was spent on the whole process. The time constraint is helpful since Fear expands to whatever size we allow. Three days of imagination running wild with everything that could go wrong gives Fear permission to be a lion-sized monster that likely began as a kitten-sized worry.

Maybe you are wishing that you didn't have any Fear? Being fearless on the surface sounds really appealing, but upon deeper reflection this thought is unwise. Ignoring Fear or not having it in the first place is foolish or even wasteful. Fear provides insight to danger and adds extra energy for survival. The deep drive to survive is a powerful force you can tap into by making Fear your friend. I ask you to intentionally begin feeling uncomfortable with this new skill to eventually harness Fear into a powerful driver.

If you always run from Fear, your life gets smaller. Consider as an alternative, to oppose your natural response and always run towards Fear. It sounds like foolishness, yet there is valuable information that Fear gives. As your friend, Fear might be warning that danger approaches, something different rounds the corner or perhaps there's an opportunity to do something that really matters. These situations and your actions, decisions and preparation all matter because what you are faced with is a challenge with important consequences.

Imagination time.

You are now a lion. Imagine that you embody this creature. What it does it feel like to look, feel, and move as a lion? Lions know how to use Fear to their advantage.

So what do lions eat? Well, those lions untrained in what to eat chase field mice and little animals for food. The result of this is much effort and very little sustenance, but not any Fear.

What if these lions knew that they were able to hunt, kill and eat bigger animals such as antelope? Instead of chasing hundreds of non-intimidating bite sized mice, there is one major antelope every week or so. As a lion, how would you rather expend your energy?

I hope you chose the one major hunt a week. Deepak Chopra claims that this principle of economy of effort from India's Vedic Science encourages, "Do less and accomplish more." This is similar to economist, Vilfredo Pareto's observation, known as the Pareto Principle, "80% of consequences come from 20% of the causes."

In hunting antelope rather than mice of life, you find the most important and sometimes scary things can make the biggest impact. The simultaneous feeling of nervousness and excitement is how to know you are chasing life's antelope. When you feel this, you invest time in the more significant things that really make a difference.

Back to the Fear Flip chart. This effective tool is useful in illuminating the edges of Fear. Oftentimes, imagination magnifies a small Fear into an obstacle too massive to conquer. The problem with big Fear is the size feels daunting and can be hard to work with and shrink to successfully address. In actuality, if you apply Fear practice and tactics, you can see the root of your Fear and see the actual, manageably small Fear.

Stoic philosopher Lucius Annaeus Seneca describes to human nature in his *Moral letters to Lucilius/Letter 13*:

> **"Accordingly, some things torment us more than they ought; some torment us before they ought; and some torment us when they ought not to torment us at all. We are in the habit of exaggerating, or imagining, or anticipating, sorrow."**

My recommendation is to actually look at your Fear with courage and discern if they are imagined or real. Then decide how to handle them as your friend Fear.

THIRTY-THREE

Fear Flip Exercise

A great way to learn the nuance of this timeless strategy is to work on only a few pieces in the final moves of a chess game as opposed to analyzing all pieces with infinite permutations of moves, which can feel too overwhelming. Let's apply that same strategy to Fear.

Think of a medium-sized Fear that's relevant to you that feels somewhat pressing now.

Really do this.

Not kidding, really. I'm going to make you turn the page.

TURN IT NOW!

. . .

For example, think of an undesired procrastination, a slight anxiety, an indecision. Let's work with something small like acorns that grow into huge oak trees.

Let's suppose you have been assigned to do a presentation in front of all of the important people in your life. Put yourself mentally in this scenario and let's grow by applying this toolset.

1. Set a timer for five minutes and write down everything about which Fear is warning you. Spend time with your worries. Notice the five-minute_limit . Notice I did not say five days. **Unchecked Fear will also fill the time container and you then allow it to metastasize to the time limit.** Keep Fear small by running at it and examining it in greater detail. In this process Fear becomes the teacher if only we look to its wisdom and our shadows. The only way to clear this challenge is through. Most people miss this critical step in overcoming Fear. When this exercise is used, it results in an epiphany of recognizing the smallness of the original Fear.
2. Remember, Fear is a gas best kept as small as necessary.
3. Itemize concerns for this presentation, e.g.: Worried about forgetting my lines.
4. Being nervous.
5. Embarrassing myself through speech or action.
6. Possible/probable failure.
7. Waste everyone's time.
8. Food in my teeth, poor appearance.
9. Sudden death.
10. Honor the 5-minute timer and stop imagining terrible and unlikely scenarios. Play with the Fear of forgetting your lines during the presentation.

Explore what you can do to mitigate this valuable Fear:

1. Video record your presentation. Rehearse it a dozen times, watch practice speeches, self-assess, and polish final product. I do this every time.
2. Practice with a test audience.
3. Write out major points on note cards.
4. Get a teleprompter.
5. With optimism, ask what's the **best that can happen**? (Notice that doesn't say 'what's the worst that can happen'; word selection is critical.)

Think, "How about instead of embarrassing myself through speech or action, I could:

1. Ask a test audience of people I trust to help with this.
2. Invite and go to the presentation with someone.
3. Practice laughing with the audience through my "mistake."

Here are some action options to make easing into Fear more effective:

1. Think to yourself, "I'm happy and excited I am feeling this because what I am about to do really matters."
2. Recall the following active aids:
3. Breathe.
4. Humbly hear the applause and compliments afterwards you are earning.
5. Visualize yourself delivering an amazing speech.
6. Smile, turning anxiety into excitement.
7. Remember the butterflies are a gift from Fear boosting you with extra energy and affirming that you are able to do something awesome!

When you think to yourself, "What if I fail?" Know that if you did the practice, received good feedback from advisors and your inner circle, you will be better next time. Even the failing is part of the ultimate successes.

My dad teaches people in his workshops to juggle. Here's is how he teaches his students.

Step 1: Drop the balls

Step 2: Pick up the balls

Very good. Now that we practiced the most useful skill in juggling, remember to pick up the dropped balls and keep learning.

See, dropping these balls wasn't so bad.

We could be so scared of making mistakes and fail to even risk dropping or making mistakes.

What if you don't do it at all? That's a bigger Fear. Don't regret what you do, only regret what you are too afraid to even try.

"Beware ye the soul-crushingness of the darkness of regret." ~B. Muka (Pirate voicing)

Also, honor why you have the Fear, maintaining your pride. Assure yourself that you are doing something that matters, otherwise there would be no Fear.

What if you think to yourself, "What if I waste everyone's time?"

Get feedback from your test audience and constructive criticism from trusted experts in the field.

What if you think, "Do I have food in my teeth?"

1. Ask a stranger or friend.
2. Do a quick mirror or phone camera check.

What if you think to yourself, "I could die from electrocution or lights falling on me?"

1. It could be your time, in which case no amount of worry will help. Death eventually comes to everyone.
2. Don't stand under the lights.
3. Don't touch the microphone or anything else electric.
4. Spend the rest of your time concentrating on what you want to go right.
5. Visualize a desired outcome - Write out tasks already completed. Congratulate yourself, you've made forward progress!
6. Focus on the points you need to hit during your talk.
7. Welcome the discomfort and enjoy a difficult and meaningful courage practice. Your world and freedom are expanding.

Here is an exercise for you:

1. Write about a situation in which you'd like to harness your Fear:

2. **Set a timer for 5-7 minutes and pull out your *Your Secret Superpower Daily Journal* and write this exercise. Careful! This exercise will change your life, especially if you practice for all major fearful events.** Expose the root of this really big Fear and brainstorm, relishing time with your worries. Notice your adjustments in just five minutes, not five days. Keep Fear small and allow only a small amount of room for your imagination to be of service. This will help you to avoid becoming overwhelmed.

3. Write out everything that comes to mind. You are finding the edge of Fear, and reducing the volume that Fear takes up. Make this resistance understood in the conscious which is removing some of its hold over you.

4. Revisit the list and take measures to reduce risk and likelihood of these dangers.

5. Spend the rest of your time concentrating on what you want to go right.

a. Visualize outcome. What do you want to happen?

b. Write out the event on paper, having already completed this challenge successfully!

c. Focus on the waypoints, which are stopping points for further explanation, that you need to hit during your talk.

d. Be uncomfortable and enjoy a difficult and meaningful courage practice. Your world and freedom are expanding. By the way, you should be a little afraid. There should be a little bit of Fear because what you are doing matters.

I applied this the first time I conducted my own skydiving course. I was honored to have my dad as one of my first students. My dad had the opportunity to fill a last-minute vacant jump spot. Our conversation went like this:

"Dad, you want to jump with us?"

"Brian, why would I ever want to jump out of a perfectly good airplane?"

"Because it's awesome and an amazing analogy for life. Everything we want in life is on the other side of life's skydives."

Remember that Fear is at its maximum when you are safe. In fact, most live through the highest danger point. End result: earned exhilaration.

Fast forward a few hours into my course:

"Brian, what's the exit like?" (An example of a buying questions for all you sales people.)

"Dad, it's like the hand of God is holding you the whole time. There is never a feeling of weightlessness unless we BASE Jump or leap from a helicopter. "

"What's the landing like?" he probed.

"Go outside and see. 80 people will be coming back to the earth peaceably, with shit-eating grins on their faces."

We jumped and he saw that I was right about all of these things.

He said, "Doesn't look so bad, like maybe jumping down two stairs."

"Dad, what did you imagine?"

"The round, PE style parachute and the World War II scenes of crashing back into the earth."

He had pictured and was afraid of something that wasn't even close to being true. In this instance, as in many, what felt like an 800-pound tiger, was really an 800-pound shadow of worry produced from Fear the size of a 10-pound kitten.

It's okay to feel Fear. I do. It's not okay, however, to let Fear run your life.

Once again, the more your practice harnessing Fear, the bigger your dreams become. The more often you are familiar with Fear, the better your relationship with Fear becomes. I believe that most people are three to five habits away from the ideal life they desire.

When Fear shows up, use it. I want you to make this a habit. Remember that stress and emergencies do not call forward your best self and performance by default. No. You sink to the lowest habitual level of your training. Practice and be ready.

When Fear shows up, use it to highlight areas of danger. The things you are afraid of force you to focus. It's not possible to get into a flow state without a bit of Fear and extreme focus, which is this amazing state where superhuman strength becomes attainable. Once you are in that moment, enjoy it. Play in it. Enjoy the true bliss and joy that happens on the other side of Fear.

Everything you want in life is on the other side of Fear.

Earn it. You must pay your friend Fear first, then you get to enjoy pure joy and success along with an amazing life that matters.

Summary of Climbing

1. Fear behaves like a gas and will expand to whatever size container you allow. Keep Fear small and manageable.
2. Use the Fear Flip chart to intelligently identify where the actual danger is, and take steps to mitigate and practice these responses when calm. Remember to spend more time with the positive outcome desired. Remember to thank God/Universe in the completion of this desire.
3. Apply mitigation techniques and find the prescription that works best for you.
4. Practice. Practice. Practice. There will be a time when all of this training and rehearsing will come in handy. I pray that you are found ready.
5. When the Fear or any of Fear's minions attack remember these three things: 1. Take a deep nourishing breath, 2. Smile to turn nervous into excitement, 3. Find Gratitude to flip the Fear switch to off. How is this situation serving me? How can this be my teacher?
6. Create an Emergency Procedure when you are calm. How will you respond to common triggers? Redefine the

emergency procedure and dial it in until it's the most effective. This will serve you incredibly well when it matters the most.

THE SUMMIT

THIRTY-FOUR

Plan for the Worst, Expect the Best

With all that said about the wedge and our choice and freedom, it's important to practice. Without engraining our ability to use the wedge to our advantage, this idea is worthless. This is a big reason why skydiving is a part of how I learned these useful lessons. While jumping at night, with equipment oxygen and a weapon, backing down was not an option. This was true courage for me. Sport jumping is one thing, but in the words of our Jump School Plaque, "The Navy: Taking the fun out of everything since 1775." Picture scrubbing the decks, and SCUBA diving but in the opposite of situation of vacation diving, with a ton of gear, ice-cold water, and visibility measured in inches. The Navy even sapped free-falling of potential joy. Jumping and flying into inky blackness with heavy equipment perverted potential exhilaration of free fall to burdensome hard work. Sport jumping is so much cooler.

I trained for a month at Otay Lakes near the California Olympic training center. Initially, skydiving was awesome and wind tunnel flying (indoor skydiving like at iFly) was like being Peter Pan.

During the day, that was very true for me. Switch the lights off, though, and holy shit! There I was at night, jumping with a rucksack, an oxygen mask strapped to my face, and a weapon. Man, that was some hard flying! The extra control surfaces of added gear, lessened overall control and suddenly, it became hard work. Then add the psychological and emotional strain of a much different flying experience, bereft of control and weighed down by extra equipment. This is why normal, sane people don't do this at night. But it does make this a covert way of commuting to work.

On this first night jump, we did it right at sunset. This was the transition from day flying to obscure, night flying. It was beautiful because we watched the sun set a second time over the Pacific Ocean. But the whole time, my imagination was festering and fueling Fear with the worry of what the completely dark landing area would be like, not to mention all of the other dangers I imagined in complete darkness.

I exited the aircraft with my instructor. No tricks were allowed if we were solo jumping, but since I was with my instructor, we got to do 60 seconds worth of fun in the sky. It helped calm my nerves because I started feeling like I had gotten away with something. (I already have my certificate so I feel safe sharing this secret with you now.)

My biggest worry was how would I know where the ground was and how to time my flair? The flair is the maneuver used to slow the descent enough to safely land the canopy to ultimately gently return to the earth.

That's not what happened. In fact, I hit the ground so hard that I tucked into forward ninja roll. My instructor buddy thought I stuck the landing with great finesse, because it happened so fast. I was already on my feet and let him think that momentarily until he took in a few details I'd hoped he'd miss. He asked me, "Why is your pack tray covered in dirt?"

Because I ate shit, we had a good laugh about it. I lived to tell the tale and realized how proud I was of myself. This landing meant that I would graduate Military Free Fall School and get to wear the gold jump wings.

Flashback to my inner monologue. Here were the questions filling me with Fear:

What would be different about jumping at night? Could I do this?

In the first instance, sport flying and jumping is a courage practice. There is nothing forcing you to jump. During the second instance at free-fall School, I didn't really have the option of walking away as it was a necessary skill for my job. This is true courage. There was no way that after the work of three years as an EOD tech that I was going to let a little night jump stand in my way. So, the Fear of failing was a bigger Fear than the skydive at night into pitch darkness. But it became this analogy for me.

When this Fear, anxiety or overwhelm hits, I could:

1. Take a breath.
2. Look at the wing, because watching the jumper fall to the earth fanned the Fear.
3. Visualize the perfect exit.

Before major sales calls, I practiced this exact same procedure.

Breathe, use this tool to reduce Fear, and then use the rest of the time visualizing what will go right. It only takes five seconds of courage to do these things.

- Five seconds to actually jump from an airplane
- Five seconds to put your shoes on to go to the gym. Once the shoes are on, you're pretty much committed to the task.
- Five Seconds of Courage is the Ted Talk from Mel Robbins. I recommend you watch her video because she's hilarious and educational.

Skydiving taught me how to do this. It's a beautiful analogy for life. As an example, from my professional sales career, sometimes because of Fear, I noticed the phone suddenly seeming to weigh a dreadful 50 pounds. Sometimes at networking events, I felt burdened by introducing myself. During the handshake, I would think, "Why does my hand suddenly feel 50 pounds heavier than usual?" Maybe you have noticed a successful or attractive person you'd like to say hi to. Why is it so much harder to talk with them?

These are some common Fears. What's a medium-sized Fear that generates resistance for you? In order to find fuel to push through that scary door, ask yourself: what's something that holds more terror? Find a bigger Fear as motivation. Failing that Fear has far worse consequences than failing the little one.

Here's an example.

Let's say you have a resistance to networking events. It's scary introducing yourself to strangers. This is the small Fear. A bigger Fear might be considering if your business fails. That's a power driver which makes saying hello feel almost silly.

Here are common Fears where picking a larger Fear for motivation and perspective can be useful and effective.

1. Being found out as an impostor.
2. New introductions.
3. Vulnerability in pursuing romance.
4. Public speaking.
5. General failure at a given task, hope or dream.

There is a study of stimuli reaction on a single mixed-martial arts (MMA) fighter and a group of untrained fighters. Both the trained fighter and a group that never experienced the stressful sounds and violence of real combat. As a result, both test subjects were initiated with terrifying, true-life combat simulations. The untrained group took twice as long to recover from the experience than the MMA fighter. The combat simulation produced elevated levels of adrenaline and cortisol. On the other hand, even though the MMA fighter had not been Fear inoculated for this specific stress, he was able to get back to calm in half the time of the untrained test subjects. This was possible, because he developed a trained Fear response, and so can you! The MMA fighter trained for and had exposure to other types of stressors. Therefore, he was able to use this ability to find a calmer approach to new stimuli. He practiced this through deliberately wrestling with discomfort. This means that as those around him were panicking and regressing to the primitive reptile brain, he was able to turn on the evolved, front brain to see more options and think more clearly.

Practice your Fear response. There may be a time in your life when you'll be glad that you did. You can learn to be the calmest person in an emergency. You'll have more options because more of your brain, your human brain, will be available to you.

THIRTY-FIVE

Skydiving Applied to Life

Before making major sales presentations, picking up the phone asking for meetings, and even speaking or introducing myself to people I really care about and on whom I want to make a good impression, I've noticed that at the surface level this feels the same way I feel right before I skydive. In fact, there's a good reason for this. Our bodies don't discriminate between worry and intense terror. Having endured both, I realized that skydiving required me to train harder than for sales calls or other factors of daily worry. Then I concentrated my mind and body into finding flow, and I could apply what I use for skydiving to my everyday life. You actually *need* Fear to get to this optimal state in the body. The difference comes in intensive courage training to hone Fear and harness it as a **superpower,** *versus* than succumbing to Fear. I acknowledge the effort it takes to mature and develop this skill. I visualize the door to the boardroom as the door to the aircraft and my emergency procedure takes over.

- I have the time for a breath, or ten breaths in this case.
- I can visualize and accurately record the best-case outcomes once completed.

- I can ask a better question like, "What's one thing I can do to make this situation a little better?" Notice I didn't say the best thing. I do this to avoid creating even more pressure.
- I can smile and remind myself this is the feeling I get before I do something awesome.
- Before I present, I can say to the audience, "Go easy on me, I'm a little nervous." People will and you have just taken some steam out of the Fear by releasing this little secret.

What are some frequent factors of your high anxiety? I ask this because in the words of billionaire investor Ray Dalio:

> **"People have a new child, and they treat it as though that's the first time anybody's had a child. But to gain perspective, you can apply it, gain that perspective of what's happened over and over, and it could be applied to anything. If you start thinking that way, it's radically beneficial. That way, when I'm referring to that is, in other words, "What is this? What one of these is it? And how do those things work? And what are my principles for dealing with it?" Then life is a whole lot easier. If you're not dealing with it that way, everything is a one-off and you'll be in the middle of a blizzard of things..."**

Are any or all of these your high anxiety events?

- Calls from "The Boss".
- Confrontations with your significant other.
- Monday blues.
- Key introductions at networking events.

- Write your own #1, #2, #3 in your journal.

"Every problem has a solution." ~Jim Koch, founder of Sam Adams Brewery

Each of these events has a solution. Options abound to reduce the magnitude of emergencies by developing a plan in optimal conditions.

THIRTY-SIX

Courage Journal

As discussed, I keep a journal and it was here that I began to see solutions to my problems. I wrote about what I wanted my life to be and distilled priceless treasure from spending time with my avalanche. How would you like to do the same? The truth is that you cannot do this alone. You will need people to help you on your journey. There's also work you can do to make sense of it all. The writing and breathing through your struggling will yield your very own sparkling gems.

It is my hope that you start to study your relationship with Fear, not shying away from shame or guilt, as they currently apply. If not now, it may happen later. Have a plan. Also, be on the lookout to help others and grow this tribe. Begin to journal in your copy of *Your Secret Superpower Daily Journal* when Fear shows up. Look at it, spend time with it first. Don't worry about finding a solution yet. The first step to improving anything is always acknowledgement. You can only improve what you measure.

This is so important. I want to share this with you again. The journal is a vital tool in harnessing Fear because it serves as an amazing snapshot of the beginning of your transformation. There are passages in my red Moleskine journal that I read from time to time to remind me how far I have climbed. Give yourself this gift.

Schedule time to journal in *Your Secret Superpower Daily Journal* . Sometimes, the act of opening your journal, with pen or pencil in hand, releases the ideas to flow. Don't worry about quality. New York Times Bestseller, Tim Ferriss recommends the following on creating healthy routine,

"**My quota for writing is two crappy pages a day.**"

Thinking about the previous quote takes the pressure away. Make it as easy as possible to spend time with your scar. Most everything worthwhile takes effort.

As world-renown artist Pablo Picasso wisely said,

"**Inspiration exists, but it has to find you working.**"

I'm not saying head blindly into the most dangerous Fear without a plan. Instead, try this approach:

1. Identify your scariest item, write it down, and circle it.
2. Thank Fear for showing us this by saying, "It is good to be scared, what is this teaching or showing me?"
3. Mitigate this Fear by choosing to breathe, standing, speaking your mantra, etc. Ask yourself, "What tool do I need right now in this moment?" Only you know the answer to this. Learn to trust your intuition when it comes to self-care.
4. Now write down your emergency procedure. In other words, how will you choose to react?
5. Visualize the perfect outcome and practice the above steps.

6. Decide and schedule the best time to "jump".
7. Jump! Enjoy the experiment and bliss of tackling and harnessing Fear.
8. Find the next scary antelope!
9. Repeat from Step 1 as needed.

THIRTY-SEVEN

Transmutation - Turn Anxiety into Excitement

To further discuss the wedge, I'd like to invite you back in time, to my high school days. I performed trumpet solos, was a featured vocalist and even played the male lead of Tony in *West Side Story*. I was on stage performing for people.

The first half of high school, I would get terrible pangs of anxiety or the butterflies. I'm not sure how this was revealed to me, but eventually I learned to put a different meaning to the feeling I experienced. What if this butterfly feeling in my chest, was actually the feeling I got before I do something awesome? What if my body was gifting me with extra energy and drive to really deliver killer performances? Pretty powerful, right?

Please consider the common advice to simply overcome Fear. Rarely is the option of tremendous inner power offered.

What. A. Waste.

What if we could learn to harness Fear and change it into a powerful force? Anxiety could become a superpower.

Did you know that our bodies cannot tell the difference between anxiety and excitement? It's the same sensation. The difference is up to us. We decide what name properly describes this visceral response.

Here is a decision point where command can be seized. This is the wedge at work. Our belief about that situation is the critical difference.

Jim Koch, founder of Sam Adams Brewery, shared a great model of how to look at Fear and danger. There are 3 types of situations:

- **Scary, Not Dangerous**; e.g., presenting on stage. No physical harm exists. Fear in this type of situation is actually worry. Worry is what we imagine to be so terrible. We can play and learn to enslave Fear to carry out our orders without significant consequences.
- **Scary, Extremely Dangerous**; e.g., walking on the roof when it's raining or icy. Not a smart idea. Fear in this type of situation is actually terror and we should trust this primal instinct. It is trying to save our lives. This is serious and not listening to Fear can get you killed. True danger doesn't give a shit about you and your ego. Be smart in such situations and honor your Fear.
- **Not Scary, Extremely Dangerous**; e.g., spring day, huge avalanche risk. This type of situation feels awesome, but actually the bomb is just waiting to explode. To ignore Fear in this type of situation is willful ignorance. This too will get us killed. Get smart, learn from experts and trust the intuition that is trying to protect your precious life.

When I'm on stage, it is a scary, but not dangerous situation. This is an opportunity to practice courage. So, one thing I can do is take a deep breath, Oh yeah that's anxiety.... Then I can smile. It's amazing what a little smile can do to let your trillions of cells know that you are safe and transmute this feeling into excitement. Practice saying this phrase: "I am/We are about to do something awesome!"

As you continue to practice this new response, you may find yourself really enjoying the way Fear gifts you with extra energy.

My point to this is, as President Franklin D. Roosevelt famously said in his first Inaugural Address,

"The only thing we have to Fear is Fear itself."

Fear itself. Not the Fear coming in ten minutes or tomorrow, but the Fear I'm feeling right now. See, anticipating more Fear to come allows Fear to fester and expand in our imaginations. I would offer that the Fear we allow to grow in our imagination are always worse than reality.

In the military's Survival, Evasion, Resistance, and Escape Course (SERE), students learn to concentrate on the pain at hand during torture. It's this anticipation of future pain, i.e. future Fear, that provides a space for Fear to expand rapidly and spin out of control. That Fear that exists in the imagination doubts with questions like:

1. What if I fail?
2. What if I forget my lines?
3. What if I'm not good enough?
4. What's the worst that can happen?
5. Who am I to lead this important project/event, etc.?
6. What if (incites the most worry)_______ happens?

I want you to see how you could just as easily imagine how great it will be when you perform at your best. You get to choose how to respond to the Fear as it shows up.

Try reversing these questions to focus the mind to see the best outcomes when the pressure is on:

1. What if I'm super successful?
2. What if I really inspire others? What if this is the feeling I get before I do something awesome (my personal favorite for anxiety and worry)?

3. What if I am good enough?
4. What if I am good/smart/talented enough to succeed?
5. What's the worst that can happen? What's the best can happen? (I want to teach the world this important reframe. Your mission is to share this. Don't just read it! Share this wealth!)
6. Who am I to selfishly hold on and not share this wisdom and expertise, leadership, solution?
7. Who will benefit from me taking this action? Don't do it just for you.
8. What am I grateful for here? What is God and the Universe teaching or challenging me with in this opportunity?

This is Fear as a coach, cheering you on, "Wake up, you're about to do something awesome!"

So, when the Fear shows up before a performance, when you're about to pick up the phone to ask for business or an appointment, or when you're about to introduce yourself to someone intimidating, remember: Breathe. Smile. It's going to be okay and it's good that you feel this Fear.

One of the coolest schools from which I graduated in the Navy was military free-fall School in California. For a month, I was paid to learn how to jump from airplanes. With my rucksack, weapon and oxygen, I "commuted" into combat with my team. We even jumped out of airplanes at night.

Thank God, I had my experience on stage to learn how to transmute anxiety, because jumping at night horrified me. This became a courage practice for me since passing on jumping into darkness wasn't an option. I had come too far to let this Fear impede my progress in my Special Operations Career. As a junior officer, I felt I had much to prove that I was worthy to wear the EOD Badge. Backing down was unacceptable.

On the ride up in the airplane we rose to 13,500 feet, or 2.5

miles. Once the side door opened and the rush of the cold air whipped through the aircraft, my anxiety presented itself. It was intense, especially as I watched the others exit the plane and darkness swallowed them. The airplane gained a few feet and it felt really odd as the previous jumpers fell away from the airplane. I was reminded that we were able to do something dangerous. So, I wrote a recipe when this feeling would strike.

Here is how I'm able to jump from airplanes:

1. Breathe.
2. Do not look at the jumper leaving the airplane. Instead, focus on the wing.
3. Imagine a perfect exit.
4. Jump!

It takes five seconds of courage to jump from an airplane. As mentioned earlier in Chapter 34, Mel Robbins explains this in an amazing way in YouTube's *Ted Talk* video, "5 Seconds of Courage."

Basically, she says that if you delay or think too much and let your imagination get the best of you, the bliss of free fall is something you'll never experience. By the way, that's a feeling like nothing else.

I now know to smile on the way up to jump. I remember to breathe and smile in the door 2.5 miles up, because I know that pure bliss is on the other side of the feeling of anxiety.

When our coach Fear shows up, we are about to do something that matters. Breathe, smile and know you are about to do something awesome!

THIRTY-EIGHT

Gratitude

"The antidote to Fear is gratitude. The antidote to anger is gratitude. You can't feel Fear or anger while feeling gratitude at the same time."
~Tony Robbins

Gratitude is a gift we can always enjoy at the time of our choosing. You may not always have time for gratitude in the moment of a quick panic of Fear. I find Fear is the greatest during periods of indecision and inaction, when we are unsure of what to do next.

There's story about the donkey torn between two identical hay bales as he stood equidistant from both. The beast of burden finds itself stuck between decisions. The donkey ultimately starves because he cannot make the decision of which bale to choose. Which way do you go? How does this show up for you? Maybe you don't know the best way to go at the moment. So, you may have time or space to worry. The Fear has the space to grow and fester like a cancer, unless, you are doing things to keep Fear small. Use the tool on this climb, gratitude. Say, "Thank You!!!"

Let me give you a couple examples. As I started writing this text,

I was quitting my very successful medical sales career. It's one of the ways I was able to build my confidence after my avalanche, save some money and learn influence and coaching skills. I walked away from what felt like a sure thing, into the unknown, to chase my dream and life's work. I developed sales mastery and coaching mastery at the same time. My heart was not in sales because I felt called to fully step into leading this movement. In the words of my friend, Papa Sunshine,

"I sold my soul to do this important work."

Will you help me spread this powerful message? I need my tribe's support in this transition.

For about 18 months I had been doing double duty, working my sales gig while constructing Fear Sherpa in my down time. This transition pressed me into the leader I need to be. I'm sure you can identify with this feeling of stress and overwhelming pressure. Maybe you identify your own transition in my experience. Exercise, family, spouse, career and leading your mission can be demanding.

This feeling of being overwhelmed was feedback letting me know that I was going to a new part of the map. What if we change the story around this feeling? This way, gratitude for growth blossoms. Truly this is what growth feels like. You know this to be true through new achievements; you must do new things. However resistance shows up, it urges you to pay attention, warning, "You have never been here before, wake up!" Nothing more, nothing less. You can intentionally choose to be excited by this opportunity to earn more of the "paint" you will use to create your masterpiece. It's how the "color" comes alive, by embracing discomfort. If you didn't feel resistance, you would be staying still, staying safe. No further exploration happens in the safe harbor, does it? Discomfort identifies the door to another place to practice gratitude when emotions like, stress, anxiety, Fear, or overwhelm show up. You are on the threshold to bigger living, and earning more consciousness, and enlightenment. Much like pain, stress and the sense of overwhelming, these things can be a door. And through this door you can press on and find bliss and truth on the other side of this challenge. Much like the smile signaling to your body that things are safe and fine, you will be okay. Gratitude can provide that same shift.

Please hear this. It is one of my hardest earned lessons. In every case, gratitude brought me through:

- Fully committing to be a Special Operations Officer.
- Surviving dive and EOD School.
- Jumping out of airplanes at night.
- Diving when I couldn't see.
- Conducting combat operations in Iraq.
- Leaving the Navy.
- Leaving the contracting world to be a professional salesman.
- Leaving sales to start Fear Sherpa.
- Addressing my biggest Fear to realize that I deserve to be loved.

The worry is biggest prior to action. The things we imagine to be the worst, are always worse in our imagination. They may feel different, yet they **ARE. NO. DIFFERENT.** I promise you, there is always truth, bliss and a bigger and happier you on the other side of that door. It's my prayer that you can embody this truth and step to the other side of the door, catching and rewarding your courage.

Gratitude can be similar. You can change impending failure into expanding and growing as an individual. The shift happens by politely saying, "Thank you for the opportunity to grow." Let me give you some examples.

I remember when there was a ton going on before I officially quit my sales job. It was stressful. I found this to be especially challenging living in this duality. Still I found gratitude in this place and said, "Thank you God for my CEO Training." When I feel uncomfortable, when I feel overwhelmed, when I feel pressure, I know I'm going to a new part of the map. The feeling of overwhelm now serves me, rather than enslaves me, because I possess the ability to change the relationship. Suffering becomes pain, even pain with a purpose, much like the discomfort of weight-lifting. This is how the muscle grows. The same is true for our courage muscle.

You may even allow a moment to say, "Good job! I'm on the path. Thank you for this gift, the ability to practice and build my business with the safety of still having a great income." So, as you look at this situation through the lens of gratitude and how this is serving you, it becomes a wonderful gift.

Here's another example.

I mentioned before that I find skydiving to be a frightening thrill. It is scary enough to create a fantastic practice for courage, yet small enough to work and play with Fear in this safe sandbox. Here I can flex and build my courage muscle. One of the things that I practice, especially while skydiving, is creating nonattached headspace on the flight up to the exit altitude. The nerves are especially intense. If you've ever ridden a roller coaster and experienced the slow methodical climb of the roller coaster, you have experienced a similar effect. Or maybe you've felt that way when you heard the sound of jet engines and the smell of jet fuel. I have incorporated that smell with the thought of doing something awesome. That feeling of anticipation and excitement sublimates from this nervous energy.

Before an actual skydive, the plane would take off, and the acceleration would push us towards the tail. We would sit almost all the way backwards because that was the most comfortable position, with your back to the front of the airplane. There were quite a few things happening that maybe we had never experienced. It was all new or newer. Our anxiety would build.

The plane would leaves the earth and we would start to feel the camaraderie with the other jumpers. Fist bumps and smiles were passed around. After a while, the plane gained more and more altitude and in crept the chill of the higher altitude. Our anxiety would increase.

I began the habit of looking out the window and giving thanks for this opportunity and view. I was grateful that I was physically fit enough to make this jump, that I had the financial means to skydive, and I had the opportunity to jump out of this airplane and would feel the exhilaration and joy of flight very soon.

Finally, when we leveled off, the anxiety built further.

Smile. This is when I would smile because choosing to do so lead my body to experience excitement rather than Fear. I practiced, and still practice, being the master of Fear. You can practice this, too. You decide to tell your body how you want to experience this, as good fun.

The door on the side of the plane opened and there's a rush of cold air. More Fear now, and it reminded me to smile and to mindfully breathe. The earth looked beautiful from this unique vantage point. I gave thanks again because from 2.5 miles up, the earth looked beautiful and we had left all of our problems on the ground. We were fully present as we concentrated on this jump. It's a new perspective. Not many people get to look out the door of an airplane. During commercial flights you get a small peephole. This was the whole side of the airplane. It was such a different experience sitting in the airplane with other masters of Fear as they prepared to play in the heavens.

The red light turned on. We fist bumped again and shared smiles. It was time to play.

Stand up, move to the edge. Take a single breath. Look at the wing, Jump! Skydiving takes five seconds of courage. There is exhilaration waiting on the other side. It's a beautiful analogy for how I believe life unfolds.

Once again, as Tony Robbins said, we cannot feel Fear and gratitude at the same time.

THIRTY-NINE

Daily Skydive

What can you do in your daily life to find your daily "skydive"? What action will you do today to build your courage muscle?

You don't need to dive out of an airplane to practice your Fear response. For me, it's getting under a heavy barbell.

Here is what I experience in weight lifting.

- Chalk on my hands.
- Grip the bar.
- Silence the inner demon by thinking, "I've got this."
- Breathe.
- Feel my strength.
- Jump!

Here are some things I suggest for practice:

- Introduce yourself to the most successful person in the room.
- Give someone a heartfelt compliment.
- Say, "Hi!" to a stranger.

- Offer to teach someone a skill at which you excel and in which they've shown interest.
- Step onto the dance floor first.
- Share a feeling.
- Start up the karaoke party.
- Ask for help, one of the scariest things to do and therefore, one of the strongest feats to accomplish.
- Speak your truth openly and honestly.

Develop a courage practice. You'll never be in a situation where you wish you were less trained. But you will always be grateful that you trained and were prepared when unexpected situations do occur.

To be trained, there is no substitute for hard work. In such moments there's no hiding. Either you did the work or you didn't. Life has a way of smoking out the liars.

FORTY

Courage Practice: Love is the Opposite of Fear

"Set aside a certain number of days, during which you shall be content with the scantiest and cheapest fare, with coarse and rough dress, saying to yourself the while: 'Is this the condition that I Feared?'" It is precisely in times of immunity from care that the soul should toughen itself beforehand for occasions of greater stress, and it is while Fortune is kind that it should fortify itself against her violence. In days of peace the soldier performs maneuvers, throws up earthworks with no enemy in sight, and wearies himself by gratuitous toil, in order that he may be equal to unavoidable toil. If you would not have a man flinch when the crisis comes, train him before it comes." ~Lucius Annaeus Seneca

I want to share with you a story about my friend, Lex. I had the pleasure of meeting him back in 2017. He literally practices the leap of faith on the world stage.

That's not a euphemism or figure of speech. He jumps over twenty feet and is the current world champion in the long jump for the Special Olympics. You see, Lex is physically blind. Yet his vision is bigger than anyone I have ever met. He may not have his sight, but this man is teaching others how to see their truth. His faith, training and love for what he does, allows him to face his Fear and demons, do something he loves, and trust that he will find bliss on the other side.

What I found most remarkable is the explanation Lex gives on jumping. He clearly articulates that he visualizes the jump and where he is in three dimensions while flying through the air. He sees the jump in his mind, runs down the runway, and is guided by the clapping sound of his guide. He left the solid ground and flew further than twenty-two feet to hold the world record for the single and triple jump.

The title of this chapter is a courage practice. You don't have to jump out of an airplane to practice courage. A defining moment arrived for me when Lex put his hand on my shoulder. The day we met, my courage practice was to introduce myself to the keynote speaker, who would turn out to my future friend.

I was intrigued by his communication because his language of choice was extremely visual. His dominant vocabulary conveys 20/20 visual ability. He uses words like "see" and "picture." It is clear he has experienced sight. His speech may catch listeners off-guard since he has lost that sense.

I had to ask him about that. His message merits repeating:

"No need for sight when you have a vision."~Lex Gillette's 2016 Ted Talk

As I'm writing this, I'm thinking how relevant that is on the Fear journey. If you have made it this far, then you have likely committed to having a new relationship with your new friend Fear. It's important to remember that you get to choose what your relationship to this Fear will be.

What do you imagine your life to be as a master of your Fear?

What does your life look like with Fear harnessed?

How will you show appreciation for your friend Fear, yet demonstrate your lordship over it?

What will you do when you slip or participate in an experience that goes differently than you hoped (otherwise known as learning and experimentation)?

These changes can instill Fear, because of a long, sometimes toxic relationship. It can feel disorienting as you change. Don't forget your visceral vision and forged faith in your end-goal. You are climbing back to the light of the living, away from the darkness in which Fear tries to hold you captive...if you let it.

Anyway, I knew that I would see for Lex and guide him that day, as we walked together. Of course, I would help. I was honored. I had the gift of sight to share. It was such a powerful moment in strength and vulnerability.

As soon as his hand was on my shoulder, I felt responsible and determined that we would get to the next spot safely.

He was the embodiment of vulnerability and strength at the same time. Actually, I would end up being the recipient of his help in a major way. He gave me a gift with his vulnerability.

A major drive for me to write this book has been to teach people to embrace their Fear because being afraid of asking for help can be deadly. In her 2012 TED Talk, author Brené Brown contends that shame exists in secrecy. People stunt their dreams or end their lives because of it. Even if this shame does not end a life, please remember the insight from Ben Franklin, "Some die at twenty-five and aren't buried until seventy-five." I have different plans for my life and yours. There's a better way.

Lex taught me a tremendous lesson that day. There is nothing weak or shameful in asking for help. Asking for help allows grace to be exchanged.

What I envision is that after all this work for a new relationship with Fear, and consequently experiencing vulnerability, without apology or justification you may ask for help. Having lived through some really scary things, I find that to be one of the scariest things of all. Showing vulnerability in a plea, "Please help me, I'm hurting," forces the truest self into the light, the self-comfortable out of sight. It hides behind answering questions dishonestly, with half-truths that preserve our public image. The true self remains in darkness in saying what people want to hear. Every time I think I overshare my brokenness with someone, it always brings me closer to that person. Strong posture is needed, knowing you have a right to hurt and there's nothing weak about it. Carefully, you may venture to show your softest parts, but only to those whom you've fully vetted and can trust.

It also takes courage to be with people as they climb through their darkness. You cannot self-rescue. It's through your vision, courage and team rescue efforts that you can help bring others back to the light. When those in need trust you, keep your integrity and to the code. That means honoring their trust in you and holding their secrets (unless there's risk of physical harm). Do not betray this precious trust conversation through gossip.

Lex helped me **see** that day.

Will you imagine something with me? Picture a table of plenty. The most delectable foods, fancy drinks, world class desserts, yet the seated guests look starving. The eating utensils are six feet long, too long for these people to feed themselves.

Picture the next table over. It has the same feast on display with the same long utensils. By contrast though, the people are happy and vibrant looking. What's the difference here? You see, even though the six-foot forks and spoons are too long to self-feed, they are the perfect tool to nourish one another by holding them for each other across the table. The company at this table thrive. The magic happens in realizing that you have something that I need and I have something you need.

That's what this book and movement are about - to be so strong as to ask without shame or guilt for help. I know this to be one of the best signs of strength.

No one escapes pain. Terrible things happen to everyone just as everyone is guilty of living imperfectly and making mistakes.

"To err is Human; to Forgive, Divine." ~Alexander Pope

Don't give up. Get back up again, a little wiser because of that last slip or fall.

As you wrestle with Fear, know that some days you will win, while other days will humble you to your Fear. That's okay as long as you try again.

Now you have more experience with harnessing Fear and can start to teach others what you've learned. These stumbles, falls and crashes are vital to our survival. The bumps, bruises and scars become part of the whole you. The events teach you so that you can start to teach others.

This metamorphosis of shame and failure into the best, freeist version of yourself allows you to contribute to improving others and therefore, the world. You may not be able to change the world single-handedly, but you can allow positive growth. You and I are part of the world and therefore, these improvements, however small and insignificant, are compounded over time to consequently change the world!

In my days with the Navy, I remember grueling workouts in which suffering was reduced considerably if there was mutual encouragement among my teammates and me. Sometimes the pain even went away. Through earned experience, you can be courageous enough to be the example, coach, or even Fear Sherpa. Strive to be a source of understanding and compassion. Without your failings and shortcomings, you would have no context to be with others through dark times. Know that this metamorphosis takes your failings and improves you. These become expensive lessons. If you don't learn and share, you've paid a massive price and haven't gained anything. It's like doing a very hard work out and then eating poorly. What's the point? The suffering you lived through now has profound meaning.

Let's talk for a second about the difference between true courage and a courage practice. Develop your courage muscle in the scary, but safe place. Most of the Fear here exists in your imagination. The consequences your Fear is telling are reversible, and sometimes they can be undone. The scary and dangerous space, where the consequences are not reversible, is something different. Your actions matter and this is the space for which you are preparing. In courage practice, always reserve the right to honor your Fear and decide to walk away. When true courage is needed, running away is no longer an option. I want to prepare you for these moments. These are the moments in which I want you to be calmer, to see more of the world that the untrained can't see. It's these moments that truly define life.

Once again, find your daily skydive. Here are some examples or discover your own!

- Volunteering to help someone else.
- Strain under a heavy barbell, a weight that scares you.
- Take on something that feels uncomfortable.
- Introduce yourself to the most successful or beautiful person in the room.
- Ask someone for help.
- Call your scariest prospect.
- Do the biggest thing on your to-do list first.
- Tutor in a field of personal expertise and passion.
- Ask for feedback from your significant other.

I hope you do these actions. I hope you add more and more uncomfortable things. As you increase this list, life expands proportionally. My desire for you is when you are tested, the fates find you ready and able to become calmer and remember to use your emergency procedures when our friend Fear visits uninvited. Already decide what to do before you feel uncomfortable, stressed or outright scared.

Picture yourself in the wild, enjoying the beauty of nature. All of the sudden, you feel it. Fear. What's different? You can feel another big animal watching, feeling you. One thing is certain, you are no longer the apex predator. Then you see the eyes of a bear or mountain lion. Do you honor your Fear and run, or do you harness it and stand your ground? Maybe you will scare them away? What do you do?

***** This story is an analogy to make a point. In survival situations please consult an expert or better yet, enroll in a wilderness survival course. *****

If you run, you will make the situation worse. This is true courage, the ability to think clearly under pressure. You cannot outrun either of these hunters, and running will entice them to hunt and kill you. Have you ever felt the primal urge to overtake someone in a race when the distance is closing? It's deeply rooted in human nature. The pursuing animal gets an extra burst of energy to close the distance. Running would be a mistake; it makes the situation worse to do so.

The best course of action would be to stand your ground.

*****Please check with the experts in your part of the world and really write out this emergency plan and don't just take my advice here. The nuanced difference could save your life. I want you to get this right because you have important work to do. *****

This is an example of testing your courage practice preparedness. Staying and fighting sometimes is the best course of action. I hope you know the best options and have practiced. Use these tools and make them an automatic response. Someday, your life or the lives of those you love could depend on your preparation. These moments in your life are waiting for you. I know I said this before and I will reiterate, there never was an instance nor will there be one in which you find yourself saying, "Man, I wish I wasn't so well prepared or trained for that."

I want you to be sick of hearing this so much that you do the work. Just like in fitness or wellness courage; in the words of Andy Frisella from his podcast, *The FMCEO Project*:

"Success cannot be bought, it cannot be negotiated, it can only be earned."

Life requires courage. It's my hope that life finds you ready for these tests. I hope it finds you as the calmest person. This is important because your calm can be infectious for good whereas panic can be infectious with devastating results. Again, choose your reaction. I want that for you.

FORTY-ONE

Fear of Our Success and Power

"No man ever steps in the same river twice, for it's not the same river and he's not the same man." ~Heraclitus

It's my hope to inspire you to use the entire palette of "color" God has gifted to you in painting your life's masterpiece. Embracing your power is accepting all the talents with which God has blessed you in pursuit of your life's purpose and work.

On Judgement Day, we will all have to answer for the unused talents gifted to us. The Lord may ask, "Why did you wait so long to use all the talents I have given you?" This is the conversation about being too afraid to play all in. To climb mountains that we could potentially fail, but to do so with joy and gratitude utilizing all of our talents. Remember, we only regret the things we were too worried to try.

Beware of the power you silently give away, at the demands of others. Why challenge this expectation of a muted version of ourselves at the convenience and comfort of others? Silent compliance suffocates your freedom to be your greatest self. But, when did you decide to be okay with this? You didn't realize what was being taken from you nor did you actively decide to be lesser. And yet, here you may find yourself, in a Fear and shame prison. A different Fear and shame prison, one that others covertly build around you, as you silently accept the oppressive box.

Day after day, year after year, concrete and cement are added to this world, a world discouraging your beauty and light, forbidding you to share all your colors with the world. You continue to paint life with the limiting black and white monochromatic bleakness. You feel blocked from embracing the entire color palette. Until you look at what others have demanded, will you actually decide.

There's a better way, if you choose to simply walk out of this prison. Here's a secret: you're the guard! Deciding to break free and fully live your biggest life can serve as a huge witness and inspiration to those in your home, community and the world. Your example, your decision and actions teach others how to live in the light with all the colors, the way God intended.

The first step to any change is awareness. Let some wind out of this sail. Remember it's okay and you are allowed to feel what you are feeling! It served a purpose at one time. The whole idea is that you are the master of your world. If it serves you–great! If your prison no longer serves you, choose to be free of it. Run towards the Fear by questioning the walls erected by others. You are choosing to begin your path to freedom and become the best version of yourself.

By vocalizing what evokes Fear and shame in you, the magnitude of the Fear and shame will decrease. Remember it is okay to feel afraid, it's a gift. It's your body's way of keeping you alive or showing you the important path you need to walk.

Share this with others. Shame and Fear lose their power when you are no longer isolated.

Who else shares your Fear?

Who has developed a better relationship with the same Fear?

These answers can release you of your shackles, if you dare ask.

Expect resistance. You may be surprised by how your loved ones try to keep you in your neat little box. Expect them to demand a smaller version of you for the sake of their comfort.

Resist! Smile and say, "No." Do not waiver with your perceived rebellion. Become your new freedom, until you can fully embrace the person you are called to be. Show more conviction on your new path than their desire to keep you in that old, colorless prison. Whoever has the most compelling vision of this future will prevail. If you acquiesce to their demands at your expense, not only will this breed resentment, **you also compromise your own integrity.**

I want to leave you with one idea. My life coach was helping me through a challenging situation with work. I was being considered for a major promotion about which I felt really uncomfortable. I expected her to comfort me and tell me it was going to be okay.

She didn't. She shared something that would change the way I viewed situations like this.

> **"I hope you are always a little afraid; it's how you know your dreams are big enough." ~Tayla Gershon**

I was blown away that day.

FORTY-TWO

Fear of Death - The Gateway to Freedom

"So live your life that the Fear of death can never enter your heart. Trouble no one about their religion; respect others in their view, and demand that they respect yours. Love your life, perfect your life, beautify all things in your life. Seek to make your life long and its purpose in the service of your people. Prepare a noble death song for the day when you go over the great divide. Always give a word or a sign of salute when meeting or passing a friend, even a stranger, when in a lonely place. Show respect to all people and grovel to none. When you arise in the morning give thanks for the food and for the joy of living. If you see no reason for giving thanks, the fault lies only in yourself. Abuse no one and no thing, for abuse turns the wise ones to fools and robs the spirit of its vision. When it comes your time to die, be not like those whose hearts are filled with the Fear of death, so that when their time comes they weep and pray for a little

more time to live their lives over again in a different way. Sing your death song and die like a hero going home." ~Chief Tecumseh

Death is stalking us. With every heartbeat, breath, and every day we are ever closer to our end. Our days are numbered and the question is, how will you meet the great inevitability?

Fear of dying is the ultimate resistance to walk through and thereby is our greatest teacher.

My friend Bryan received an incredible gift, T-minus 60 days due to kidney and liver failure. Most of us will not receive this insight of how much longer we have on this planet. Death will come to us, and when it does, will we beg more time? Or will we live a life in accordance with the Chief Tecumseh quote, and sing our death song and return home? Death will not be negotiated with, despite our pleas for more. "What about all the time I already gave you?" Death will say.

Therefore, we must be ever vigilant and live life honoring the resistances we discover. Will you wait until the end for death to be an amazing teacher? With the insight and mindset shift you now have, how will your life different. If you had 60 days of life left, what worries and annoyances could you release? How would you spend your time? What would you want to leave behind? Who would you forgive and reconcile with? For whom would you express gratitude and love? What experiences would you enjoy?

Write your answers in *Your Secret Superpower Daily Journal.* Those bucket list items are transformed from dreams to goals the second those are inscribed.

*****Place due dates next to them, and make it happen. Don't wait until death knocks on your door to figure this out. Tell your friends and family and invite them along or simply to be your accountability partner in its completion.*****

Die Empty.

"Dost thou love life? Then do not squander time, for that is the stuff life is made of." ~Benjamin Franklin

Our days are finite. The number of times we get to see a sunset, share time with our loved ones, are all numbered. These things are precious and death as our teacher highlights why we need gratitude to enjoy these set number of special moments.

A game changing book on this subject is *Die Empty: Unleash your Best Work Every Day,* written by Todd Henry.

My favorite quote of mine from this reading is:

"The most valuable land in the world is the graveyard. In the graveyard are buried all of the unwritten novels, never-launched businesses, unreconciled relationships, and all of the other things that people thought, 'I'll get around to that tomorrow.' One day, however, their tomorrows ran."

Having spent time with this book, you possess the working knowledge to run towards our friend Fear. Fear and death, if harnessed properly, are daring us to shed the old limiting beliefs, do uncomfortable things, and realize our greatest potential. As a veteran tasked with the job of running towards the explosive hazards, I knew what I was willing to exchange my life for my men, my family and loved ones to do my duty. I ask you, what are you willing to lay your life down for as your duty if called upon? The answer to this yields true freedom.

"To begin depriving death of its greatest advantage over us, let us adopt a way clean contrary to that

> **common one; let us deprive death of its strangeness, let us frequent it, let us get used to it; let us have nothing more often in mind than death... We do not know where death awaits us: so let us wait for it everywhere. To practice death is to practice freedom. A man who has learned how to die has unlearned how to be a slave." ~Michel de Montaigne**

I'm not ready to leave yet. There's so much left in me that needs to be shared before I'm eased into my body's final resting place. Please help me in spreading this message of hope and mastery by practicing courage, commanding Fear, supporting avalanche survivors, and painting your life's masterpiece.

Summary of the Summit

1. You are not your thoughts nor are you your inner monologue. Speak kindly to yourself to regulate your Fear, anxieties, and addictions.

2. There's a space between stimulus and reaction where we have the freedom to choose what to do next resides. It's my hope that you find your way to expand this wedge to find your calm even when the storm rages outside.

3. Find a daily "skydive," a safe way to hone the courage muscle for the time when running away could be the worst or nonexistent option. Remember when the stress hormones hit, the natural tendency is to revert to baseline training.

4. Life will test us! Prepare now with these tools to become calmer and respond better. The choice is yours; either do the work or don't in preparation for these moments of testing.

5. Develop a courage practice to rehearse your reactions. Write your emergency procedures when you are calm, but remember to write and practice. Also, these need to be redefined to be made more accurate and useful.

6. The discomfort, anxiety, Fear and pain remind you that you

are in a new place, doing things that matter. Find pride and self-respect in earning your paint for the masterpiece that is your life.

7. In addressing our inevitable Death, our friend Fear shows us the path to fully living our lives to the max. It is seldom the easiest path, but the journey that allows us to die empty of all our best ideas, relationships and a life without regrets

8. Checklists are vital tools for making difficult decisions when it matters most. Write out your emergency procedure before you need it for the repeating high-value Fear in your life. As in the OODA loop, know you can save valuable time in considering reactions before the "airplane" crashes to the earth.

***How will you apply this mindset to your life?

9. Keep a log of progress with *Your Secret Superpower Daily Journal.* Work the process into being a masterpiece through firing, readying, then aiming. With each new documented shot, you become more accurate.

***What's something that you want to dial in regarding your daily practice?

10. The most important item, the single priority (notice I didn't use the plural) is sometimes the scariest. Develop the habit of seeking the highest leveraged to-do-list item. Don't delay until tomorrow that which is better done today. Eventually, the most important item can become the most effortless. Usually it isn't the starting point, though. It takes courage to decline the interesting, not most-vital item daily.

Every day, use *Your Secret Superpower Daily Journal* to identify the answer to this question: "What's the most important thing to do today?" If you feel Fear, good. This means you are accomplishing things that matter. With the compound effect in mind, keeping the streak alive by everyday doing something that scares you. You'll like the results, I promise.

About the Author

Brian Muka is the founder of Fear Sherpa. Fear in the hands of a master becomes a superpower; Fear in the hands of the untrained can be deadly. Join Fear Sherpa Movement and learn to harness Fear.

About the Author

EPILOGUE

You did it!

You finished the book! Most people don't do that. Most people buy the book and don't finish Chapter 1, because they don't start reading immediately. Guess what, the dusty book on the shelf doesn't add any value. You did it! You didn't let it collect dust. Thank you for joining me on this journey.

The truth is, I needed this book as much as you needed it. As you read in my story, I felt buried alive in an avalanche. Some of this was my doing, and some of it was done to me. Unfortunately, I let Fear steal the part that I could control from me. It is my hope that you learn from that.

It was my Fear of being thought an impostor, that I didn't have the "it" of being a member of the Special Operations community. It was a thought virus and I allowed it to fester. This was a cancer of self-doubt, self-loathing, shame, and guilt, and all of it was predicated on this unfounded Fear. I could have put the poison in its proper place five minutes after I thought it.

The teacher appears when the student is ready. I wasn't quite ready to learn this hard-earned lesson and I certainly never would have volunteered for this path. Today, I'm so thankful that I have a story and message to share with you.

I realize now that in order to lead this movement, I had to summit and return home again with the treasure that you are holding in your hand right now. How to cope and learn from long term Fear was the missing piece I needed to understand how our powerful friend Fear can be harnessed. This story and the purpose behind keeping my red Moleskine journal was to find meaning in the suffering that I endured. I didn't know it then, but that log would be the start of this book. The purpose was and is to help you with your life's climb to your realized potential. Fear is the gatekeeper and can be a great friend, coach, and North Star.

A developed superpower for me is my choice in what to do with Fear in the moment. Now you have the tools to develop your own superpower.

You learned in this guidebook, the power of other breath, expansions of your wedge, the space between the stimulus and the response, and now you have an answer to the question:

"How can I become calmer?"

What you hold in your hands, this book, I had to complete as much for you as for me. I needed to share this story because other people have been and will be blown up and called to walk a difficult road by life's avalanches. And if nothing else, I could be a guide who has been to that summit will be with you in your journey, and help you through it. It's how I made sense of what could be the most epic failure of my life thus far, exiting my Navy career. Everything came along and I missed the waypoint. I had a great track record until then, picking a target, working diligently and executing many years of training and experience. This time was different, though. I felt my best missed the mark. And so, I was left to wonder, "What do I do now?"

I would like to smooth the way and ease the hard climbing that life throws at you. This finished work is a relic of that, a physical manifestation of my desire to help you to find meaning in your avalanche. It's funny the way that this all works. That epic failure would turn out to be my life's work.

Every single time I help someone like you understand Fear better, understanding the ramifications of being mastered by Fear in terms of shame and guilt, I realize that the path to get here is worth it. This darkness I carried in Iraq, the darkness I carried in Virginia Beach, the darkness that I carried after I was no longer a Special Operations officer anymore all makes sense now.

God or the Universe had a different plan for me, a better plan. This movement that you are joining is meaningful. At the very least, I can leave this earth knowing that I left this ripple, a footprint in the sand, of what I have earned and how to help others with their struggles.

I can leave the earth today knowing that I made a positive impact. I now know, because you are holding the completion of my toiling in this guidebook, how to handle Fear. This is the lynchpin to the outrageous life that you deserve. Awaken the sleeping dragon that lies dormant within you. Practice courage, find ways to be uncomfortable and step into the power of being courageous enough to harness this untapped source of energy.

It may feel scary now. Fear is going to come up again. You did not start this journey to cure Fear. That would be a waste of precious, usable energy. Instead, play and wrestle with Fear. Sometimes you will win and be the master of Fear. Sometimes, you will not. As a guide, I fall too and it's ok. It's good in some ways because you become smarter with every fall, or as I call it now, "An interesting experiment that doesn't go the way I thought it would."

In the experiments that don't kill you, you are given the gift of trying again. Decide to get up again, but this time, be wiser by the lessons honed by this uncomfortable experience. You are more familiar with Fear and this hard-earned wisdom helps with future victories. You can now aid others in their engagements with Fear. In the words of Sun Tzu's *Art of War*:

"Know thy enemy."

When you feel an uncomfortable pang, that is anxiety or Fear. Know that you have gotten to the edge of knowledge and comfort on the map. With your courage practice and ability to press on into that world of pain or discomfort you earn the paint to define an unexplored area of the map. It's my hope that you earn the colorful paint that will authentically reflect how brilliant, multi-dimensional and unique you are in the masterpiece of your life.

Seek bigger mountains to climb, grander peaks and goals for which to strive, knowing Fear has been tamed into a friend. Fear can focus us and propel us forward. Truly, Fear in the hands of a master becomes a superpower. Fear in the Hands of the untrained as you know is deadly.

My hope for you is lift of the best parts of you and become the commander of Fear. May you find and help others who need this work. Remain open to other masters and Fear Sherpas in the making. Encourage masters-in-training to just keep going. Join a team and contribute to a rescue team that keep an eye out for troubled members who've lost their way or are digging out of their avalanches.

Let us show the world what to do with Fear. You no longer have to live in Fear of Fear. Harness your Fear and be Fear's master. Discern what Fear is telling you. Is it worry and in our imagination? Or is this a threat that needs to be addressed now? You get to decide what to do with this thought. By deepening our relationship and understanding we can use or shed Fear, in order to complete our life's mission.

Thank you for reading and being part of Fear Sherpa. Go forth now and free the world from the slavery of limitless and unbridled Fear. Liberate those imprisoned and enslaved.

To you, the newest member of Fear Sherpa, climb to your best self, harness your Fear and guide others.

BIBLIOGRAPHY

Foreword

W. Clement Stone and Napoleon Hill, *Success Through a Positive Mental Attitude* (Gallery Books; Reprint edition June 12, 2007 (original 1960)).

Quote by John H. Secondari from *Saga of Western Man,* directed by Helen Jean Rogers, written by John Hermes Secondari, (aired February 23, 1965, ABC News/Secondari Productions).

Avalanche

Chapter 1 This is My Gift to You

Concussion, directed by Peter Landesman, written by Peter Landesman, Jeanne Marie Laskas (based on the GQ article "Game Brain" by), featuring Will Smith, Alec Baldwin, Albert Brooks, (25 December 2015; LStar Capital/Scott Free Productions/The

Cantillon Company/The Shuman Company/Village Roadshow Pictures), DVD.

Quote from Rumi: https://www.goodreads.com/quotes/801814-don-t-turn-away-keep-your-gaze-on-the-bandaged-place

Chapter 4 Introducing Our Friend, Fear

Viktor E. Frankl, *Man's Search for Meaning* (Beacon Press; 1 edition June 1, 2006).

Chapter 5 Hire Fear, Do It Now, and Make This Powerful Ally Work On Your Behalf

John A. Sheff, *Salt from My Attic* (Mosher Press, 1928).

Chapter 6 Naming Your Fear – We Are Not Our Fear

Maleficent, directed by Robert Stromberg, Linda Woolverton (screenplay by), Charles Perrault (based on "La Belle au bois dormant" written by), featuring Angelina Jolie, Elle Fanning, Sharlto Copley, (30 May 2014; Roth Films, Walt Disney Pictures), DVD.

Quote from Captain Flint from "XXVIII," the tenth episode in the third season of the STARZ series *Black Sails.*

Chapter 7 Birth of the Fear Sherpa

Hurt Locker, directed by Kathryn Bigelow, written by Mark Boal, featuring Jeremy Renner, Anthony Mackie, Brian Geraghty, (31 July 2009; Voltage Pictures (presents)/Grosvenor Park Media (in association with)/Film Capital Europe Funds (FCEF) (in association with) (as F.C.E.F. S.A.)/First Light Production/Kingsgate Films/Summit Entertainment (produced in association with)), DVD.

Reference to CrossFit: Glassman, G. (2010). *Defining CrossFit by Greg Glassman.* [online] CrossFit Journal. Available at: http://

journal.crossfit.com/2010/12/glassmandefining.tpl [Accessed 11 Feb. 2015].

Christopher McDougall, *Born to Run: A Hidden Tribe, Superathletes, and the Greatest Race the World Has Never Seen* (Vintage; Reprint edition (March 29, 2011)

Viktor E. Frankl, *Man's Search for Meaning* (Beacon Press; 1 edition June 1, 2006).

Moleskine® is a registered trademark of Moleskine Srl a socio unico - https://us.moleskine.com/company

Base Camp

Chapter 8 Assemble Your Rescue Team and Make a Plan

James W. Pennebaker and Joshua M. Smyth, *Opening Up by Writing It Down, Third Edition: How Expressive Writing Improves Health and Eases Emotional Pain,* (The Guilford Press; Third edition (July 15, 2016)

Chapter 9 The Inner Adventure and Our Thoughts – Do Your Inner Monologue and Imagination Serve You?

Quote from Peter Drucker from Steven Kotler and Jamie Wheal, *Stealing Fire: How Silicon Valley, the Navy SEALs, and Maverick Scientists Are Revolutionizing the Way We Live and Work,* Dey Street Books; Reprint edition (May 8, 2018)

Lao Tzu, *Tao Te Ching,* CreateSpace Independent Publishing Platform (January 22, 2018)

Chapter 10 Fear of Our Success and Power

Marianne Williamson, *A Return to Love: Reflections on the Prin-*

ciples of a Course in Miracles, (HarperOne; Reissue edition (March 15, 1996)

Quote from George Bernard Shaw: https://www.goodreads.com/quotes/536961-the-reasonable-man-adapts-himself-to-the-world-the-unreasonable

Quote from Robert Lynd: https://www.goodreads.-com/quotes/830198-it-is-easier-to-believe-a-lie-that-one-has

Chapter 11 Prep the Battlefield

Jim Collins, *Good to Great: Why Some Companies Make the Leap...and Others Don't,* HarperBusiness; 1st edition (October 16, 2001).

Napoleon Hill, *Think and Grow Rich,* Sound Wisdom; Reprint edition (December 13, 2016) (original 1937)).

Chapter 12 Look Inward: Find Your Own Answers

Quote from Rumi: https://www.goodreads.com/quotes/801814-don-t-turn-away-keep-your-gaze-on-the-bandaged-place

Ice

Chapter 13 "Breathe, Mother F*#&er" - Wim Hof

Wim Hof and Justin Rosales, *Becoming the Iceman,* Mill City Press, Inc. (November 22, 2011).

Chapter 14 The Breath: Wim Hof and the Ice Bath Method

Brandon Powell, quote shared with the author.

Wikipedia, s.v. "Nitric Oxide," last modified August 1, 2019,

14:47 (UTC), https://en.wikipedia.org/wiki/Nitric_oxide

Youtube, "PNTV: The Oxygen Advantage by Patrick McKeowns. December 11, 2017, https://www.youtube.com/watch?v=iWXDdnsELOw

Chapter 15 The Breath That Saved My Life

Steve Wentz, owner of Blue Skies, quote shared with the author.

Chapter 16 Reptile Dysfunction

Youtube, "Wim Hof The Iceman Demonstrates His Breathing Technique with Lewis Howes", October 30, 2016, https://www.youtube.com/watch?v=RW1C_3OXhEs

Chapter 17 Ask Better Questions

Quote from the podcast *The Advanced Selling Podcast*, https://advancedsellingpodcast.com/.

Quote from Ken Follett: https://www.goodreads.com/work/quotes/1576118

Michael A. Singer, *The Untethered Soul: The Journey Beyond Yourself*, New Harbinger Publications/ Noetic Books; 1 edition (October 3, 2007).

Chapter 18, Get Rescued!

Meru, directed by Jimmy Chin and Elizabeth Chai Vasarhelyi, featuring Conrad Anker, Grace Chin, Jimmy Chin, (14 August 2014; Music Box Films, DVD.

Wikipedia, s.v. "2015 Sundance Film Festival," last modified April 22, 2019, 02:14 (UTC), https://en.wikipedia.org/wiki/2015_Sundance_Film_Festival

Youtube, "Meru Official Trailer #1 (2015) Documentary Movie

HD", July 20, 2015, https://www.youtube.com/watch?v=qdWzTqyMtSU

J.K. Rowling, A. Singer, *Harry Potter and the Order of the Phoenix (Book 5)*, Arthur A. Levine Books; 1st edition (July 1, 2003)

Chapter 19, Story A and Story B

Mark England, owner of Procabulary, quotes shared with the author.

Chapter 20, Fear as a North Star

Winston S Churchill, *The Story of the Malakand Field Force*, Dover Publications (March 18, 2010) (original London 1898)).

Quote from Peter Drucker, "Managing for Business Effectiveness," *Harvard Business Review*, from the May 1963 issue, https://hbr.org/1963/05/managing-for-business-effectiveness.

Chapter 21, Worry is Not a Performance Enhancing Drug

Dr. John Muka, quote shared with the author.

Sun Tzu, *The Art of War,* Filiquarian; First Thus edition (November 7, 2007).

Chapter 22 Inner Monologue: Devil On Your Shoulder

Quote from Tim Ferriss, Benjamin Hardy "By Asking Himself This 9-Word Question, Tim Ferriss Changed His Life," *Forbes*, December 13, 2017, https://www.forbes.com/sites/benjaminphardy/2017/12/13/by-asking-himself-this-9-word-question-tim-ferriss-changed-his-life/#26a9264c5df5.

Quote from Socrates: https://www.goodreads.com/quotes/

search?utf8=%E2%9C%93&q=the+unexamined+life+is+not+worth+living&commit=Search

Scripture from New International Version Holy Bible, Zondervan; Lea edition (August 21, 2018).

Quote from the podcast *The Advanced Selling Podcast,* https://advancedsellingpodcast.com/.

"Unleash Your Inner Strength™ Tony Robbins Quotes, Incantations, and other Resources," https://unleashyourinnerstrength.com/2010/04/09/tony-robbins-quotes-incantations/.

Quote from David Hackworth, from Tim Ferriss, *Tribe of Mentors: Short Life Advice from the Best in the World,* Vermilion (2017).

Quote from author, Brian Muka.

Chapter 23 Prevent the Hurricane in the First Place

"The Tim Ferriss Radio Hour: Meditation, Mindset and Mastery;" in *tim.blog,* a blog by Tim Ferriss.

Quote from author, Brian Muka.

"How to Cage the Monkey Mind (#175)" in *tim.blog,* a blog by Tim Ferriss.

Underwater

Chapter 25, The Day I Ran Out of Air Fifty Feet Underwater and Was Trapped

James Nestor, *Deep: Freediving, Renegade Science, and What the Ocean Tells Us About Ourselves,* Eamon Dolan/Mariner Books; Reprint edition (May 5, 2015).

Leanna Garfield, "The founder of Bulletproof Coffee plans to live to be 180 years old," *Business Insider,* April 13, 2016, https://

www.businessinsider.com/bulletproof-coffee-ceo-dave-asprey-wants-to-hack-death-2016-4.

Chapter 26 Stimulus -> Freedom -> Reaction

Viktor E. Frankl, *Man's Search for Meaning* (Beacon Press; 1 edition June 1, 2006 (original 1946)).

Youtube, Will Smith, "What Skydiving Taught Me About Fear | STORYTIME", April 26, 2018, https://www.youtube.com/watch?v=bFIB05LGtMs.

Chapter 27, Compound Effect

Quote from Jim Rohn: https://www.goodreads.com/quotes/56225-i-will-take-care-of-me-for-you-if-you

Climbing

Chapter 28, Climbing with Wim Hof

Vibram Five Fingers Shoes are a trademark of the Vibram Five-Fingers LLC.

Chapter 29, The Crux

Ryan Holiday, *The Obstacle is the Way: The Ancient Art of Turning Adversity to Advantage*, PROFILE BOOKS; Main edition (2001).

Quote from Jack London: https://www.goodreads.com/quotes/2851-i-would-rather-be-ashes-than-dust-i-would-rather

. . .

Chapter 30, Emergency Procedure – OODA Loop by Colonel John Boyd

Atul Gawande, *The Checklist Manifesto: How to Get Things Right*. Picador; First edition (January 4, 2011).

Chet Richards, *Certain to Win: The Strategy of John Boyd, Applied to Business*. Xlibris, Corp. (June 24, 2004)

Chapter 32 Fear Mitigation – Fear as a Gas

Sun Tzu, *The Art of War,* Filiquarian; First Thus edition (November 7, 2007).

Fear Flip Chart from Fear Sherpa, www.Fearsherpa.com

Deepak Chopra, "Law of Least Effort" January 6, 2010, Awakin.org, http://www.awakin.org/read/view.php?tid=666

Will Kenton, "Pareto Principle," updated July 19, 2019, Investopedia.com, https://www.investopedia.com/terms/p/paretoprinciple.asp.

Aly Juma, "Seneca on the Folly of Groundless Fear," January 14, 2016. Medium.com, https://medium.com/swlh/seneca-on-the-folly-of-groundless-Fear-db65dc6afb26.

Chapter 33 Fear Flip Exercise

Brian Muka, author's quote

The Summit

Chapter 34 Plan for the Worst, Expect the Best

Mel Robbins, "How to Stop Screwing Yourself Over," TED Talks, June 2011. Ted.com, https://www.ted.com/talks/mel_robbins_how_to_stop_screwing_yourself_over?language=en.

. . .

Chapter 35 Skydiving Applied to Life

Ray Dalio, *Principles: Life and Work*, Simon & Schuster; 1st edition (September 19, 2017).

Terri Evans, "Boston Beer Co.'s Jim Koch on Self Reliance," November 30, 2011. Entrepreneur.com, https://www.entrepreneur.com/article/220792.

Chapter 36 Courage Journal

Rachel Gregg, "Passion and Practice: Tim Ferriss & Neil Strauss's Tips for Better Writing," 2014. CreativeLive Blog.com, https://www.creativelive.com/blog/tim-ferriss-neil-strauss-writing-advice/.

Quote from Pablio Picasso: https://www.goodreads.com/quotes/30296-inspiration-exists-but-it-has-to-find-you-working

Chapter 37 Transmutation – Turn Anxiety into Excitement

Quote from President Franklin D. Roosevelt: https://www.goodreads.com/quotes/search?utf8=%E2%9C%93&q=The+only+thing+we+have+to+Fear+is+Fear+itself&commit=Search

Mel Robbins, "How to Stop Screwing Yourself Over," TED Talks, June 2011. Ted.com, https://www.ted.com/talks/mel_robbins_how_to_stop_screwing_yourself_over?language=en.

Chapter 38 Gratitude

Tony Robbins, "Tony Robbins: 'Gratitude Is the Solution to Anger and Fear' "Making a difference in any measurable way grabs me," November 29, 2016. Medium.com, https://medium.com/thrive-global/tony-robbins-gratitude-is-the-solution-to-anger-and-Fear-c3fa819825c.

Papa Sunshine, quote shared with the author.

. . .

Chapter 40 Courage Practice: Love is the Opposite of Fear

Quote from Lucius Annaeus Seneca: https://www.goodreads.com/quotes/977535-set-aside-a-certain-number-of-days-during-which-you

Lex Gillette, "Wings Are Just a Detail," TEDx San Diego, November 25, 2016, https://www.tedxsandiego.com/wings-are-just-a-detail-lex-gillette-at-tedxsandiego-2016/

Brené Brown, "Listening to Shame," March 2012, https://www.ted.com/talks/brene_brown_listening_to_shame?language=en.

Quote from Benjamin Franklinhttps://www.goodreads.-com/quotes/85334-many-people-die-at-twenty-five-and-aren-t-buried-until

Alexander Pope, *An Essay on Criticism, Part II*, Franklin Classics (October 16, 2018 (original 1711)).

Quote from the podcast *The MFCEO Project Podcast*, https://andyfrisella.com/blogs/mfceo-project-podcast.

Chapter 41 Fear of Our Success and Power

Quote from Heraclitus: https://www.goodreads.com/quotes/117526-no-man-ever-steps-in-the-same-river-twice-for

Tayla Gershon, life coach, quote shared with the author.

Chapter 42 Fear of Death – The Gateway to Freedom

Quote from Chief Tecumseh: https://www.goodreads.-com/quotes/1025817-so-live-your-life-that-the-Fear-of-death-can

Quote from Benjamin Franklin: https://www.goodreads.com/quotes/search?utf8=%E2%9C%93&q=Dost+thou+love+life%3F+Then+do+not+squander+time%2C+for+that+is+the+stuff+life+is+made+of&commit=Search

Todd Henry, *Die Empty: Unleash your Best Work Every Day,* Portfolio; Reprint edition (April 28, 2015).

Quote from Michel de Montaigne: https://www.goodreads.com/quotes/36604-to-begin-depriving-death-of-its-greatest-advantage-over-us

Epilogue

Sun Tzu, *The Art of War,* Filiquarian; First Thus edition (November 7, 2007).

CPSIA information can be obtained
at www.ICGtesting.com
Printed in the USA
FSHW010509121119
64009FS